Healing in His Wings: Honoring and Embracing God's Promises

Patricia Simon

Rejoice Connection

Hammond, Louisiana

Dedication

To my supportive husband, Alton, who continues to encourage me in all things.

Acknowledgments

To my friends and family and all who graciously accepted my telephone calls for Bible reading and prayer.

To my incredibly wise and gifted editor, Norma Jean Lutz.

Contents

Preface 7

Introduction 11

Part I 27

Healing 27

Love and Reconciliation 27

Jesus the Healer 35

The Name of Jesus 45

The Holy Spirit and Authority 51

Where Did Sickness Come From? 69

Prayer, Fasting, And Order 77

Rest 95

Obedience, Faith and Believing 101

Walking in Faith 109

The Fear of The Lord—Reverence, Honor and Obedience .113

Humility 123

Self Restraint 129

Part II 135

Hindrances and Barriers to Healing 135

   Pride 137

   Doubt and Unbelief 142

   Unforgiveness 145

   The Spirit of Fear 147

   Stress and Worry 151

   Discouragement, Disappointment, or Bitterness 153

Self-Reliance 156

Disobedience and Sin 159

Demonic Oppression 161

Other Strongholds 164

General Barriers 167

Part III 169

Believe and Receive Your Healing 169

Proclaim God's Word for Healing 169

Praise Your Way to Healing 170

The Medical Community for Healing 171

Believe and Receive 172

Conclusion 173

About the Author 177

Preface

Between 400 and 500 BC, during the time of Malachi the prophet, God had a harsh warning for the people of Judah. They had forgotten who they were. They were a covenant people who were chosen to usher in the government of Jesus. However, their apathy and indifference concerning the Levitical ordinances had summoned the wrath of God, who would now call the prophet Malachi to speak to them in a series of warnings.

The priests of the land had become complacent and unprincipled in their relationship with God. There were problems of false worship, marriage problems, questioning God's love for them, and great emphasis on the handling of sacrifices, specifically tithes and offerings. They had forgotten the way of the Patriarchs and the Mosaic practices which had been in existence since its inception in 1500 BC almost 1100 years earlier. They did remember the Levites methodical (religious) way of instituting the tithes and offering but had abandoned the heart of true worship in their sacrificial giving. They were bringing to the altar blemished animals for sacrifice.

God is a God of holiness. Holiness requires true worship and reverence. In the core of this established order of sacrificial giving was a three-fold system. This system would allow Judah, in proper form and reverent hearts, to worship God through giving. It would also give Judah the opportunity to trust God for their provision. Thirdly, it was prophetic of the greater offering and sacrifice to come. This could not be done half-heartedly. The animals brought before God represented love and honor to Him, but was also a picture of the perfect sacrifice, Jesus. The animals had to be perfect. How had Judah lost sight of its significance?

Malachi the Prophet

Here, at this juncture, the prophet Malachi came on the scene with stern warnings of Judah's corruption. They had made a mockery of worship and polluted the altar. Malachi told the people that God was so filled with wrath that He was considering striking the earth with a curse. Amid all this fury though, God took notice of a remnant of believers who still had hope. Believers who were still enthralled in witnessing the coming of the King. This righteous remnant who feared God, aroused the compassion of God for His people, for there were prophecies yet to be fulfilled. Even so, it was paramount for the Priests, and all others, to understand the heart of true worship and the beauty of sacrificial giving.

God told the prophet Malachi to prophesy about the two messengers.

"Behold, I send my messenger, and he will prepare the way before me. and the Lord who you seek, will suddenly come to the temple. even the Messenger of the covenant, in whom you delight. Behold, He is coming." says the Lord of hosts.

Malachi 3:1

Two Messengers

We understand the first messenger to be John the Baptist, and the second to be Jesus. As Malachi prophesied about the first coming of Jesus, he also intertwined aspects of the second advent (The Return of the Lord). He went on to tell the priest that Jesus would purify the sons of Levi and purge them as gold and silver that they may offer to the Lord an offering in righteousness. Then the offering of Judah and Jerusalem would be pleasant to the Lord, as in the days of old.

Malachi spoke again concerning the righteous remnant who feared the Lord. They spoke to one another, and the Lord listened and heard them. The Lord said, "They shall be mine. On the day that I will make them my jewels, I will spare them as a man spares his own son who serves him." This remnant would be key to fulfilling the redemptive order of God's Genesis 3:15 decree.

Though Malachi completed this writing with judgement, employing second advent language because of Judah's offense, he also offered hope to those who feared God. The Sun of Righteousness shall arise with healing in His wings (both advents). He brought light to not only penetrate the darkness of sin and disobedience, but He illuminated the earth with grace, power, and light.

Encased in the first advent's plan of salvation is redemption, forgiveness, spiritual and physical healing, unspeakable joy with complete restoration and reconciliation to Father in Heaven. So then, believers would be able to enter in the presence of God with Jesus as High Priest.

Until that time, Malachi needed to encourage Judah to continue in the Law of Moses. If the law continued as prescribed during that dispensation, then the people would be more observant about service, honor, worship, and relationships. At this stage, it was incumbent that the people understand the importance of presenting a pure and unblemished offering before the Lord. It was all about worship.

Our attitude relating to the things of God helps to determine our progress and success in life. It is significant when implementing strategies for Kingdom work including personal and spiritual growth; especially in the area of healing because healing may not always be immediate.

We all want miraculous, instant healings as we see most often in Scripture. But that might not always be the case. There are times when healing might be progressive which could be discouraging and challenging to our faith. In this case, having the right attitude and spirit toward the things of God will play an important role in how we respond to our healing process.

Intimacy with God

Take time to develop intimacy with God. Remember also, repentance and forgiveness could be a factor in delaying the healing manifestation. Spend time getting to know God that you might better understand how to serve and trust Him.

For now, these passages in Malachi show that God was reinforcing the formula for abundant living. He instructed Malachi to guide Judah and Jerusalem in the way of tradition and obedience. Malachi proclaimed that God would send Elijah the prophet (first and second advents) before the great and dreadful Day of the Lord. And He will turn the hearts of the fathers to the children and the hearts of the children to their fathers (Malachi 4:5,6).

John the Baptist, in the spirit of Elijah, would come to stimulate the world with the ordinance of water baptism as creation transitioned from the Old Covenant to the New. The earth would also witness the birth of Christ followed by baptism with the fire of the Holy Spirit. As the blood of Jesus reconciles us to God, and the Holy Spirit is received, the hearts of the father and of children will, by faith, be returned one to the other, and henceforth to God. Under the direction of the Holy Spirit, our hearts were turned, and we can now serve God in this new dispensation.

The righteous remnant of Malachi's day, who yet believed, moved God to remember His merciful plan to send the Sun of Righteousness with *healing in His wings.*

Introduction

L ong before my bout with Covid-19, I had been thinking a lot about sickness among believers and pondering why in the Body of Christ, we were not benefiting from promises contained in the Word; specifically, sickness, in relation to divine healing and wondering whether we truly believed God's Word. Nine-hundred years before Jesus came, His Word declared in Isaiah 53: 5, "By His Stripes, we are healed." About twenty years after His death, it tells us in 1 Peter 2:24, that "we were healed."

I'm not sure we understand what that means. Many decided the usage of *healed* signifies spiritual healing—a renewal as a result of atonement. Others believe *healing* is indicative of an all-inclusive dynamic which includes both spiritual and physical healing; that when our sins were forgiven, we were healed in every possible way.

There is a direct connection between falling into sin and falling into sickness. When we were liberated from the curse of sin, we were freed from the curse of sickness. How each of us responds to these truths might differ. The variable that determines our successful healing, or manifestation, is unique depending on God's plan and purpose for us, as well as our faith and our belief system.

Whole Healing

Psalm 103:3 tells us He forgives all our iniquities and heals all our diseases. One might suggest that this is a general attribute of God and not necessarily a simultaneous redemptive occurrence. Yet, further examination as indicated in 1 Peter 2:24 plainly indicates an all-inclusive atoning deliverance where propitiation facilitated the reconciliation and rendering whole healing for the mind, body and soul. The wrath of our Holy God was placated thereby reversing the curse of sin and death, catapulting us into newfound inheritance as sons and daughters of the Most High.

Though this is in plain language, it's difficult to grasp the full scope of the truth of these Scriptures because we look around and see many are sick. What else do we need to know? When on earth, Jesus healed all, except those who did not believe. These healings and deliverances were clear examples of our forthcoming abilities and privileges as believers. Yet, here we are in the year of 2023 and are still challenged with not having knowledge and understanding of Christians receiving their healing according to the Word of God, even though most believe.

One hindrance is our inability to rightly divide God's Word and to see clearly that it's God's will for us all to be healed. We need to see that it's our own fears, doubts, and ignorance that keeps up in bondage. Of course, the answer is not as simple as that, but it is a starting place. There are many variables. some of which are addressed in Part II *Hindrances and Barriers*. Regardless, the Gospel of Jesus Christ offers healing for all mankind, and we need to know how to access our God-given rights.

Like most Christians, I am struggling to understand. We're praying that God would give us insight so that we, as the body of Christ, may be catapulted into the realm of being physically fit and healthy to do God's work. Also drawing others to

Christ, not denying the power of God but having full assurance of His supernatural abilities. And as we tread this journey, we will continue to gain more wisdom while holding on to these truths. As the apostle Paul says, "Let us not stay carnal minded," (which hinders our growth) but let us move from milk to solid food where we can acquire an understanding of how to receive our healing that has already been given to us through the blood of Jesus (Hebrews 5:13, 14).

My Healing Testimony

God healed me from a stroke I had had years earlier. After the stroke episode, I was mildly paralyzed for a few days. Afterward, I went to therapy for six weeks and was slowly mending. But I lingered in terror as I experienced high blood pressure and a general feeling of unwellness. The fear, coupled with high blood pressure medicine, lasted for ten years. About four years ago I was finally able to stop taking the blood pressure medicine that had held me hostage for ten long years after the stroke. To be free of medicine was paramount for me—a strange joy, yet inexpressible fear.

While on the blood pressure medicine, I was in constant turmoil. One pill made my pressure too high, the other, too low. I clung to that medicine, though with total resentment. The fear of another stroke plagued me. Part of my daily routine was checking my blood pressure throughout the day. Most of my eating, planning and activities centered around my blood pressure reading. I absolutely abhorred it. I'd been praying and asking God to please help me get off the medicine for I felt as though it was more hurtful than helpful.

During that time, my prescription's strength was lowered a little at a time. This is the tenderness of God. He knew I might not have enough faith to quit taking the medicine outright, so God weened me from the medicine, enough so that I was able to hear an inner voice say, "You don't need the medicine anymore. Let go of fear and you'll have the courage you need to be free of the medicine."

I let the medicine go, though in great fear and trembling but was able to muster some faith in between. Scariest thing ever! After that, every unusual thing that occurred in my body convinced me that I was having another stroke. One day, I was certain the stroke attack was imminent. There was a strange feeling at the back of my neck. I remember my doctor telling me that if I experienced pain in the back of my neck to get to the doctor. The stroke I had had, was a hemorrhagic assault which occurred at the base of my brain, so any unusual pain or feelings could be a sign of another attack. On this day, there was this pull on my neck. It terrified me!

I was determined to trust the Voice that told me I didn't need the medicine, yet I felt drawn to find that medicine and take it for I had never thrown it away. It had only been one month since I had stopped taking it. I considered going to the doctor that day but was desperately trying not to fall into fear. There was a fight inside of me that wanted to walk in faith and trust God. I tried to act as normally as possible, but on the inside I felt doomed.

Later and still trembling in fear, I prepared for bed thinking I might not wake up the next morning for my neck still had this uncomfortable pull. As I attempted to unzip my sweater in the back, I noticed my hair was tangled and caught in the zipper which was creating the unusual pulling to my neck. I laughed and cried for days! I felt as if this was a test of my faith. After that incident, I felt strong and encouraged to walk out my faith to be free of medicine. From that day, I began to immerse myself into healing Scriptures and searching for resources on divine healing.

I was reflecting on all this right before I got sick with Covid, thinking about sickness and as Christians, how to address the challenge by acting on God's Word. I was asking spiritual questions about sickness as it relates to healing Scriptures in the Bible and the work of Jesus. I even began writing this book thinking that maybe I could start a healing forum where believers could come together and ponder some of the questions I was asking. There seemed to be a disconnect. As Christians, our sicknesses and medications do not align with Bible truths and promises.

Then Came Covid

As I began to write and think more about this, I remembered that next day would have been two years that I had been off medications. That evening, my husband came home and announced that he tested positive for Covid-19. Though fear set in, I felt confident that our daughter and I (she was twenty-five and has Down syndrome) would escape this terrible epidemic. After all, she is known as the prayer warrior among friends and family. And ever since my stroke episode, I had been studying healing Scriptures and conversing about the power of God. Surely, we would be kept from this thing.

At that time our life group had been reviewing various types of prayers in order to help enhance our prayer life. I had felt my prayer time and attitude of worship was good. Though many times I needed to be reminded concerning commitment and complacency. Our daughter is loved by all and loves all except when she tells me she does not care and a big melt-down occurs. It is a sweet, but crazy, scene.

These thoughts invaded my mind as part of my defense therapy to help guard against a Covid attack. Even so, Covid attacked us both and was brutal. Some days I felt death at my door. I experienced a death-like taste in my mouth, and the feeling that my breath was being sucked out of me. I was unsure if my Scriptures were helping to heal as I felt unconscious half the time. Maybe somewhere in the depth of me, the Word would call out. I couldn't pray, I didn't have the strength to think. But the Lord is merciful.

On one of my weakest mornings, with my body feeling as though it had been pounded in the grave with only my hands hanging out, there was a whisper in my soul to text certain people in my life to pray for me. I protested because I didn't have the strength to pick up the phone, nor was I accustomed to asking people to pray for me.

One reason it was difficult for me to ask for prayer was because during my journey after the stroke, I felt as though God was teaching me and establishing me. I was under a mandate to contact individuals by phone and read Scripture during my recuperation. Talk about awkward! And in the beginning, it truly was. Then it became fulfilling.

I learned great discipline in listening and in managing time. I scheduled different individuals at certain times. It became routine to share scriptures of encouragement, conduct general Bible reading, and then closing each session with prayer. This was the arrangement for years.

Because of this routine, it became difficult for me to ask for prayer. Sometimes we get accustomed to praying for others, or doing for others, and it becomes strange when we need to ask for prayer or whatever. It is okay to ask for prayer or seek help from friends or family when needed. You're not weak or any less a Christian because you need to ask for prayer. We don't need to whine over every little scrape; but by the same token we do need to guard against tendencies of self-reliance and pride. (This is discussed in more detail in Hindrances and Barriers).

Reaching Out

So here I am on day three of Covid and am being directed by the Holy Spirit to text others to pray for me. I managed to text one individual. I put the phone down, protested, and then texted the next. This was the pattern over the six texts that went out that morning. Two were group texts to my prayer friends. I knew I had to obey the tugging in my spirit even though it seemed to be an impossible exercise. When I was done texting, I felt myself slipping away, because the pain in my head and my body, along with so little breath, was far too intense!

As I drifted all I could think about was my soul feeling satisfied that I was able to heed and complete the task of contacting the people to pray for me. When I reflect, I realize it was the prayers of the saints, the blood of Jesus, and the power of the Holy Ghost, that saved our daughter, my husband, and me from death during the early days of Covid.

I had no idea what was going on in my daughter's room during that time. I only know that she was not well. She's usually an early-rising busybody. I hadn't seen her in days. We talked to our physician via video and managed to get prescriptions that my husband was giving to each of us. (Thank God, his bout with Covid was mild.)

One morning around 2:00 a.m. I was awakened, felt disturbed and directed—practically ushered—to go to my office. At this point, I felt even weaker than the day I had to text people, so I was unsure how I would maneuver this feat. As I began to walk to the other room, I was wobbly, and my weakened bones trembled. I could barely see. Undisputedly, I know angels were holding me up! When I turned to go into the office, I spotted my chair. My arms stretched forward to latch on to it long before I was near it. I almost fell. As I sat down, my eyes tried to focus on papers and other items to try to understand why I felt such an overwhelming need to go to my office.

The White Envelopes

The only thing that caught my eye was the stack of long white envelopes sitting on the corner of my desk. I remembered my daughter had been placing these envelopes here. Each one contained five dollars representing her tithes from whenever she got paid. They had been stacking up on my desk. Typically, we would deposit them in the bank and pay the tithes from her debit card. I had been so busy lately that I hadn't had time to make the deposit. Meanwhile, they had been piling up, falling to the floor with other items piled on top. I didn't really think anything of it other than, "I need to get to the bank."

But as I sat there, suffering under the woes of Covid, I compared these white envelopes that were being tossed around on my desk, to the people of Malachi's day. What I was doing was no different. As I pondered this, I wanted to rectify the situation because I honestly felt I was near death. I did not want to die with my daughter's tithes piled on my desk.

As mentioned, I had not thought about it, but at this point something just felt wrong. As I sat there in pain, trying to clear my thinking, there seemed to be a loud, whistling of a steam locomotive noise outside my window. I'm not sure what it was or where it came from. I have never heard it since. Some people see beautiful bright lights and heavenly things in a near-death experience. But I heard the *death railway wagon* coming for me. All I knew was I wanted to do something about my daughter's tithes that had been accumulating on my desk. The whistling noise moved me to go ahead and count the tithe and pay it from the account. There was an urgency; I knew I absolutely needed to do this before my last breath. As I attempted this seemingly difficult task, death loomed.

I struggled to go to my bedroom to get my bankcard, then struggled to return to the office. Inputting the information to pay the tithe was exhausting. I couldn't see clearly and the webpage for my church was resisting my payment. I kept trying. I had never before had trouble with this. Covid pain wasn't helping.

After numerous attempts, the thing was completed. I was confused and trying to understand what God wanted me to see in all of this. What I was able to glean from the experience was eye-opening.

In the beginning, after our tests revealed we had Covid, there was a window of opportunity for me to stand on God's Word and declare our healing. I was more drawn to believe in the diagnosis rather than to rise up and take authority. To command the symptoms (which were mild at that stage) to flee. Also, after many years of delaying my writing, the fact that I was writing about sickness and healing prior to getting sick with Covid seemed strange.

I believe my complacent attitude toward our daughter's offerings gave the devil a legal place to attack. Also, the fact that I was writing about the people of Judah and their apathy concerning God's offering seemed hypocritical. As I reflected on my attitude concerning the tithe envelopes, I was saddened that I had been so cavalier and not more attentive about the things of God. In my reckoning of this, I wept at the realization that as our daughter diligently paid her tithes, she entrusted me to be a good steward in the handling of the matter. Now typically, this might seem like a small matter, but because of the way I was directed to address this during a time when I felt as if my life was nearing the end, I knew that I needed to pay attention.

As I reflected on all this, I remembered wanting to title this book *Divine Healing,* with no mention of the book Malachi. But the Holy Spirit had me go back to see what was happening in the last book in the Bible preceding the arrival of Jesus on earth. In retrospect, I think it was God's way of correcting me regarding my complacency. However, I didn't see it until I was half-dead with Covid. In the physical, all I saw was that God had given me a new title and had given me some insight about Judah during the time of Malachi.

Armed with fresh knowledge, enthusiasm, and confidence that God was instructing me in this, I was just going to skip along and write my book. I was blinded by the fact that God wanted me to be able to recognize my negligence as being similar to that of Judah. Sometimes, God will put something right in our face and we still don't see it. I was bent on the narrative of Judah's failures and lack of commitment and message of judgement, and yet did not see my own lack of attention to duty.

As mentioned, I did not see any wrong in having the tithe envelopes sitting around, propping my feet on my desk, sometimes with the envelopes falling around. But as I sat in my chair, weeping at the revelation of what was shown to me in my weakened state, I asked God to forgive me. I prayed to become more vigilant and to be more attentive to God's work. These things matter to God!

Remember, we have an enemy accusing us before God day and night. When we are disciplined and developed, we are more functional and better effective at winning souls. Ultimately that's the purpose. God does not need our daughter's money. It's not about that. It's about order and reverence. It's about correction and being sensitive and receptive to be used by God. It starts with obedience and reverence to the things of God.

Repair the Breach

Because I was in error, the enemy saw an opportunity to kill me while I was in a weakened state. I heard the whistling and noise of a freight train outside my window during my weakest Covid episode, with Holy Spirit guiding me to repair the breach. At that time, I perceived this event to be a warning of impending death that was about to occur at any moment. God is a God of justice, so when we open that door, we're liable to see or hear anything. This unusual experience is indelibly etched in my mind. Subsequently, the noise subsided and the spirit of death—or whatever the thing was—vanished.

I'm thankful that God loves me enough to correct me by whatever means necessary. Whom the Lord loves, He corrects (Proverbs 3:12).

As I sat there and continued to reflect on the unusual things that had happened that morning, my spirit was urged to write. I got a pencil and paper and began writing these principles that came to my spirit.

Tithes and offerings must be done in proper worship and in order. As mentioned in my introduction, it's not about giving money to God. It's about honor and remembering the greater sacrifice, Jesus, who is our First Fruit without blemish. Meaning we put God first, with a willful and obedient heart.

- Paying tithes encourages us to embrace the covenant of faith between us and the Father where we come to acknowledge that He is our Provider.
- Be holy, for I am holy (1 Peter 1:16).
- Pray and care for the things of Israel.
- Put God first in all things.
- True worship and honor come from the heart.
- Remember the Tabernacle of David. All nations need to experience the power of God unto salvation (the Gospel of Jesus), and to have a heart for prayer, praise, and worship individually and collectively in this time of grace where Jesus is Lord. Don't forget to assemble. Attend church. Jesus told us we'll do greater things under the New Testament promises.
- Be vigilant to not entertain idols. This refers to anything that we harbor or hold too close to our heart, esteeming it to be more important than God. Oftentimes deceptions and traps are common in this area because we fail to recognize the traps of the enemy.
- When you are doing work for God, stay committed. Don't be slothful or take it lightly, doing it half-heartedly without enthusiasm. Be diligent, exude peace, and be filled with the joy of the Lord. Be sensitive to the Holy Spirit that He

may give you the guidance you need. Above all, have a heart of reverence toward God.

As I sat there, looking around my office, I wondered if there was something else that I had neglected to do. I didn't have the strength to go back to my bed, so I pulled another chair over in front of me and stretched out my legs to rest. Again, I reflected on how God had me read the book of Malachi to correct me and to teach many things that early morning hour.

In my chair, I dosed off in bewilderment, with Covid still plaguing. The sense of looming death had subsided, along with the whistling train noise. To this day I'm still trying to understand what happened during that time. One thing's for sure, God healed my family.

I ached for my brothers and sisters who were still struggling in pain or in the hospital, because I felt connected. My heart was heavy as I thought about those who were mourning and grieving their lost ones. Like many others, I wanted desperately to do something.

In the beginning, many helped with making masks and sending food to elder facilities. Sometimes, basic care and prayer is all you can do in certain situations. We ordered Bibles for distribution during that time, but the mandate was to stay put and stay safe. So, we gave Bibles to neighbors, family, and friends. Though we wanted to give to others, we had little contact.

Nearing my post-Covid stage, though still having random flareups and physically exhausted, I had this spiritual energy and believed this would be an opportunity for unbelievers to know Jesus. I cried a lot because I wasn't sure how to navigate soul winning at this juncture, because people were confused and fearful. The fear and anxiousness were not just due to Covid, but also due to political unrest.

Blindness and Confusion

There was a kind of blindness and confusion in the world. There were groups of people dying and families suffering, while many groups were protesting for various interests. There was unprecedented division around the world. We witnessed death, violence, suffering, fighting, fear and more confusion. Yet in all this, still there was hate. The thing was still alive! That thing called pride. We invite sickness and stress because we don't abide by the words of Jesus to "Love God and love each other" (Mark 12:30,31).

Many argued concerning the source of Covid's spread. Sure, Covid had a tangible culprit but what about our spiritual condition? Could it be that hate had manifested itself into true, physical world-wide sickness where people died? Jesus said to love God and to love each other. We disobeyed! We know that hate and disobedience can bring sickness. Loving was difficult for many during this time of political unrest and turmoil. Ironically, loving and caring for one another was probably the balm we needed to truly heal. Not just physically but mentally, emotionally, and spiritually as well. Pride kills.

As I mentioned earlier, sometimes as Christians we lose sight of who we are and believe we're doing okay spiritually, not recognizing that deceptive traps have caused us to blindly drift away from truth and holiness of God. The way I mishandled the tithes was evidence that my assessment of my spiritual walk was off kilter. I was unaware that I was not as engaged as I should have been. I'm learning to be more watchful to the things of God.

Sickness is not from God; however, when we open doors in disobedience or ignorance, the devil will come in and bring whatever chaos he can. The devil brings sickness. He plays upon our weaknesses. God is a God of justice. We might experience natural consequences as a result of sin; but God also gives us a way of escape from the wiles of the devil.

Thank you, Jesus, for recourse that we can ask for forgiveness and abide by Your word. "Submit to God, resist the devil and he will flee from you" (James 4:7). Stay away from the traps. We are first told to submit. When we surrender, we get the strength we need to resist the devil. Be sensitive to the whisperings of the Holy Spirit. Correction from God is vital to spiritual growth.

Now, to address my earlier concerns of the disconnect between the frequent occurrence of sickness on the part of the believer, and the divine exchange where we understand that Jesus bore our sickness at the cross (Matthew 8:17); I was even more determined to complete this writing despite my month-long interruption due to Covid, plus other sicknesses during this writing. And many healings.

It's my hope that we will all gain greater perspective concerning healing and the divine exchange through prayer, Bible study, and the power and direction of the Holy Spirit. Let's learn and grow with optimism as we experience God's love for us; so much so that we'll be convinced that it is His will for us to be healthy and whole. We'll explore the truth of the gospel to see what the Word is speaking to us.

It's my sincere prayer that you may grow in your spiritual walk by reading *Healing in His Wings: Honoring and Embracing God's Promises*.

Part I

Healing

Chapter 1

Love and Reconciliation

If it had not been the lord who was on our side…

Psalm 124:1

The old, rugged cross symbolizes beams of beauty when we absorb John 3:16. For God so loved the world that He gave His only begotten Son, that whoever believes in Him should not perish but have everlasting life.

Furthermore, we learn in Romans 5:6-8, that when we were still without strength, in due time Christ died for the ungodly. For scarcely for a righteous man will one die, yet perhaps for a good man someone would even dare to die. But

God demonstrates his own love toward us, in that while we were still sinners, Christ died for us. Humanity will never fully grasp the love God has for us.

...to know the love of Christ which passes knowledge; that you may be filled with all the fullness of God.

Ephesians 3:19

Through the reading and hearing of His Word, we can gain the faith we need to trust Him and gain some sense of the love and compassion God bestows upon us. One thing I've learned is that when we have honest and pure love for others according to Galatians, our lives will closely resemble and reflect the love God has for us.

But the fruit of the Spirit is love, joy, peace, patience, kindness, goodness, faithfulness, gentleness, and self-control.

Galatians 5:22

Jesus told us to love God and love each other. The two are perpetually linked. Sometimes, we forget that.

As New Covenant believers in Jesus, we have access to the full Scripture. We can read of God's love for us and experience His love in a variety of ways. Old Testament, believers, were not as privileged. Relationships with God were dependent on the High Priest. Many of the prophets and kings would hear from God, but for the average person this was not so.

That's the beauty of the Cross. God has not changed. His covenant with His people has changed. Jesus is our High Priest now. Through the blood of Jesus, God has given to us the helmet of salvation. The apostle Paul also referred to it also as the hope of salvation whereby the great exchange has already been activated, and we can joyfully look ahead to the promise of eternal life.

Incorporated in that exchange lie many benefits. We can legally step into our inheritance and begin to experience other New-Covenant promises. God not only laid our iniquities upon Jesus, but He blessed us with every spiritual blessing (Ephesians 1:3). In this exchange, through the power of the blood of Jesus, we were reconciled to God so that when we confess Jesus as our Lord and Savior, we become part of the Body of Christ. By faith, we are better able to receive the promises and blessings of God. Through the power of the Holy Spirit, we are in a better position to appropriate the authority He has laid upon us.

God gave His Son to us because of His great love for us. Throughout the pages of Scripture, we see the power of God's love. After Adam and Eve sinned, they became cognizant of their nakedness. God, in His tender mercy, made tunics from animal's skin to clothe them. He could have let them stay in the garden in their sin forever, but His love was so great for them, He sent them out to give them and all of mankind the opportunity of eternal life through the shed blood of Jesus.

So, in addition to an opportunity to live in eternity, He has given us abundant life as we live here on earth. "Blessed are those who mourn, for they shall be comforted" (Matthew 5:4). "He heals the brokenhearted and binds up their wounds" (Psalm 147:3). The knowledge that God cares for us when we are hurt, disappointed, or have sinned, is remarkable. He loves us that much and His love, in itself, heals us because Scripture tells us that it was by His stripes--his sufferings—that we are healed. He suffered because of the love He has for us. Still, we have to believe, receive, and obey. His love for us compels us to be healed.

The Apostle Paul tells us that Christ suffered once for our sins—the just for the unjust—that He might bring us to God (1 Peter 3:18). Yes, Jesus brought us back to God! We were created to live in peace with God, even though our early parents allowed Satan to infuse doubt and conflict within their economy in order to snatch their God-given authority. Yes, our negative choices can facilitate the enemy's plans. The thief was successful in his purpose. He managed to cause separation between God and man while securing authority for himself.

But God's unending love for us determined that He would reconcile us to Him. This love catapulted the plan for redemptive hope. A hope that would be carried little by little, time after time, through the years. God's remnant people, by His spirit, was essential to carrying out His plan. This remnant would pass on what they could, in the form of tradition and the written word. Despite famine, wars, defeat, captivity, disappointment, suffering, persecution and death, hope was carried. The remnant was spiritually sustained enough to bring the promise of hope into fruition. The fruit being Jesus, bearing total reconciliation. The magnificence of hope fulfilled and the result being reconciliation of God, our creator, to his children is unfathomable. And though we don't comprehend, we are yet witnesses to this extraordinary event. Hope is grand, in that it is able to lift, encourage, and motivate people to the finish of things.

How do we today respond to this remarkable love of God and His passion to reconcile with us? The thing is, He is still longsuffering concerning our sinful behavior. He is waiting for many to confess Jesus as Lord and Savior.

He is not slack concerning his promise, as some count slackness, but is longsuffering toward us, not willing that any should perish but that all should come to repentance.

2 Peter 3:9

The apostle Paul tells us in Romans,

We rejoice in God through our Lord, Jesus Christ, through whom we have now received reconciliation.

Romans 5:11

Our reasonable response should then be to acknowledge that the same ministry of reconciliation that was laid upon Jesus has fallen upon us.

Therefore, if anyone is in Christ, he is a new creation; old things have passed away; behold all things have become new. Now all things are of God, who has reconciled us to himself through Jesus Christ, and has given to us the ministry of reconciliation, that is, that God was in Christ reconciling the word to himself, not imputing their transgressions to them, and has committed to us the word of reconciliation. Now then, we are ambassadors to Christ, as though God were pleading through us: we implore you on Christ behalf, be reconciled to God.

2 Corinthians 5:17-20

As believers, we can share the good news with others, that God has restored peace where the enemy has wreaked turmoil.

He sent healing and the hope of eternal life when the devil tried to keep us in oppression. His grace has positioned us to journey to the finish line as we prepare for the return of Christ. His mercy wraps us in the best of linen. The kind where the fibers are well formed and sturdy, yet soft to the touch. The kind of linen to where no snag, rip, or tear will diminish its ability to hold, comfort, and carry us even when we lose sight of who we are and become discouraged. When we become so downtrodden by life's situations, the fabric of His mercy continues to heal and restore us when we call out to Him.

Throughout Scripture we are told to declare His Word. There is a finish line. The Apostle Paul tells us to run this race, not as one beating the air but as one looking to finish and reap the reward (1 Corinthians 9:26). Paul's race is about winning souls; for us to remind others of this great ministry of reconciliation. To holler, when necessary, "Be reconciled to God!" There's healing in hollering! The hollering might not always be verbal. It might be the result of someone who is walking in the Fruit of the Spirit while their countenance exudes the faithfulness of God. In that posture, we're able to "Have our conduct honorable among the Gentiles (unbelievers) that when they speak against you as evildoers, they may, by your good works, which they observe, glorify God in the day of visitation." 2 Peter 2:12.

"Seek first the Kingdom of God, and His righteousness; and all these things will be added to you" (Matthew 6:33). Forget about what you need for a moment and share the Gospel. There's love, power, and healing in sharing God's Word. The Bible tells us that the Word of God is medicine to our flesh (Proverbs 4:20). Share the Word and impart healing for yourself, and the hearer.

So then, after the Lord had spoken to them, He was received up into heaven, and sat down at the right hand of God. And they went out and preached everywhere, the Lord working with them and confirming the word through the accompanying signs.

Mark 16:19-20

There're miracles to behold in soul winning.

The righteous shall flourish like a palm tree, He shall grow like a cedar in Lebanon. Those who are planted in the house of the Lord Shall flourish in the courts of our God. They shall still bear fruit in old age; They shall be fresh and flourishing, to declare that the Lord is upright; He is my rock, and there is no unrighteousness in Him.

Psalm 92:12-15

Chapter 2

Jesus the Healer

The shed blood of Jesus has facilitated every need and opposition we might encounter including healing. He bears all and is portrayed in the gospels as our Savior and Lord who cares about our wellbeing. He wants us whole! As He carefully orchestrates His journeys and short time with us, He makes it clear that He wants to take our hurt and our pain and does not want us to be oppressed by the devil. He's the healer, the one who brings liberty to those in bondage.

And when He stood up to read, the scroll of the prophet Isaiah was handed to Him. Unrolling it, He found the place where it was written: "The Spirit of the Lord is on Me, because He has anointed Me to preach good news to the poor. He has sent Me to proclaim liberty to the captives and recovery of sight to the blind, to release the oppressed, proclaim the year of the Lord's favor."

Luke 4:17-19

Jesus went on to tell the people, "Today this Scripture is fulfilled in your hearing." The people of Nazareth rejected

Jesus' message at this juncture. They were offended because of his poor family background and the authority He carried.

Jesus is filled with wisdom and as we see in the book of John, He's preaching about being the bread from heaven. In Nazareth, they're familiar with His upbringing, so they took offense at His teaching, merely judging by what they thought they knew. The Bible tells us that Jesus did not do many mighty works there because of their unbelief. Mark tells us He laid hands on a few sick people and healed them, and He marveled because of their unbelief (Mark 6:6).

Jesus came to bring healing. He was the healing balm they needed then, and He is the balm we need today. Just because they did not believe does not diminish the healing power of God. It simply decreases their opportunity to receive healing—or anything else for that matter. Other verses tell us that Jesus went on to heal all who were sick. He could perform no miracles where unbelief dwells. When we believe, all things are possible. Simply believe. Believe in the healing power of God through the blood of Jesus. Believe Jesus is the Son of God, the Bread of Life! Believe He is the Word and faith comes by hearing the Word. He can do no mighty work when unbelief is in your heart. You cannot receive, where unbelief abides.

In Luke 4, Jesus delivers a message of hope and healing. This discourse resonates with those who believe in divine healing. For we latch on to Scriptures relating to healing, deliverance, and being set free from oppression. We're filled with unspeakable expectation when we read that God heals all our diseases. We also find healing in verses that speak of love and prosperity. There's healing in passages that encourages us and reminds us to, "Fear the Lord and obey His Word"

(Proverbs 3:7,8; 4:20-23). The Gospel of Jesus gives us keys to unlock an endowment that equips us to serve. We want to be healthy to be able to minister to others. We want to utilize the tools God has given us for effective soul winning. Jesus wants us healthy so that we are able to testify, to promote the Gospel, and to glorify God. His love continues to sweep over us that we might have whole health and abundant life as we make strides toward that glorious day. Being intimately aware of God's love for us is healing!

Notice in the Luke passage, that the Spirit of the Lord was upon Jesus. He explained that He was anointed to heal our hurt. In Acts 10, Peter reinforces this message when he speaks to the crowd at the house of Cornelius. He tells them:

> *You yourselves know what has happened throughout Judea, beginning in Galilee with the baptism that John proclaimed: how God anointed Jesus of Nazareth with the Holy Spirit and with power, and how Jesus went around doing good and healing all who were oppressed by the devil, because God was with Him.*
>
> Acts 10:37,38

His healing ministry in that day and even now, continues to demonstrate the magnitude of how God wants wellness and deliverance for all. These acts of healings and deliverance is God's message of hope, reminding us that it doesn't matter if you are like blind Bartimaeus (Mark 10) or possessed with a demon like the naked man living in the tombs (Matthew 8), healing is for all! He anointed Jesus to care for us.

The shed blood of Jesus still nurses our wounds. He is still our great Physician and is sitting at the right hand of God mediating on our behalf. What a lovely vision! Though we were healed by His stripes, we're learning how to appropriate our faith that we might receive and activate that which was given us. We must recognize that God deals with us individually. Our healing might be immediate, by process, might be tied to unforgiveness or some other variation pertaining to our spiritual growth.

Satan is busy. Remember his method of operation is to kill, still and destroy (John 10:10). But the Healer is anointed with power to give abundant life. Let's choose to believe the Word of God so when the enemy comes calling, we can say, "Flee, devil, in the name of Jesus! You are trespassing. Be gone!"

Is it that simple? Not really. But it can be. Let God's Holy Spirit build you up so that you can begin walking in the kind of faith where you will confidently call that spirit of infirmity out and tell it never to return. You can rebuke Satan and his symptoms. You will come to understand that you have a greater power living inside of you than the evil foe that's manipulating individuals and the whole world (1 John 4:4). You have no power without the power of the Holy Ghost and the presence of God in your life.

> *But you shall receive power when the Holy Spirit has come upon you; and you shall be witnesses to me in Jerusalem, and in all Judea and Samaria and to the end of the earth.*
>
> Acts 1:8

Jesus' fame went throughout all Syria, "and they brought to him all sick people who were affected with various diseases and torments, and those who were demon possessed, epileptics, and paralytics and He healed them" (Matthew

> 38

4:24). This passage gives us a vivid account of how the actions of our Lord and Savior translated His eternal love for us by way of healing and wholeness. We also see the Messiah, not under duress or pain, but a willingness to restore peace and faith in God's economy of believers -- A demonstration of wellness that Father God had already proclaimed for His children. During the Crucifixion, as the lamb endured a beating for us in an act of selfless obedience, believers witnessed a continued humble willingness to heal the hurt, as He prepared the world for restoration and reconciliation to almighty God.

As we continue to walk in the promises of the word of God, we see Jesus in His Sonship, in His Majesty, we see Him as High Priest, King of Kings, and Lord of Lords. In all this, we yet see Jesus as Rabboni, our Master, our Teacher and Healer. Though we now live in post-ascension era where believers can step up to their anointing, we can witness the same supernatural power of Jesus working as we experience miracles for ourselves and for others. We tend to cling to the Gospels and can very much relate when Jesus was presented as Son of Man and Teacher; however, He now sits as High Priest. We worship Him as He continues to mediate on our behalf.

When we read the Gospels, oftentimes we wonder what it must have been like to live in the days of Jesus. Imagine, a downcast like Blind Bartimaeus in your town. He calls out to Jesus to have mercy on him while being quietened and hushed by onlookers so as not to bother Jesus. In his lovingkindness, Jesus takes notice of Bartimaeus. Above the whispers and hushing of, "Be quiet man," Jesus hears Bartimaeus cry out: "Son of David, have mercy on me!"

Despite the others trying to hinder his attempts, Bartimaeus calls out again. In the depth of his blindness, he knew Jesus. He heard about Jesus, and he believed! He called out in faith. He wasn't concerned about what anyone thought. He became indignant in his plea. Not so indignant as to harm or hurt, but desperate to experience the move and power of God. When Jesus called him out, he threw off his cloak.

This act was a monumental expression of faith for his identity was wrapped in this cloak denoting him as a person with special needs and requiring aid. He was willing to surrender all to depend on Jesus for his healing.

Jesus said to him, "What do you want me to do for you?" Bartimaeus replied to Him saying, "Rabboni, that I may receive my sight." Jesus said to him, go your way, your faith has made you well." Immediately he received his sight (Mark 10:46-52).

What a time! Even though we read about all the miracles and have knowledge of Messiah, Jesus told us that our time (New Covenant) is better than the Old because we have better promises.

Truly, truly, I tell you, whoever believes in Me will also do the works that I am doing. He will do even greater things than these, because I am going to the Father.

John 14:12

As He transitioned to Heaven, He promised to send the Holy Spirit. So here we see that we're able to do greater works:

- We have the power of the Holy Ghost living inside us.

- We have Jesus at the right hand of God mediating on our behalf.
- We can pray in the Name of Jesus at this stage, where we could not before His ascension.
- We have better mobility in terms of travel and technology.
- We are simply better equipped to spread the Gospel and see signs and wonders.

The important thing is that word got out about the miracles of Jesus. Scripture tells us that blind Bartimaeus heard about Jesus. The word was out. The word is still out. Jesus is our healer. We were healed at the cross! Declare your identity, have faith, and receive your healing in the Name of Jesus! Make certain you're not plagued with unforgiveness, bitterness, or some other barrier that might obstruct the flow of your healing. (See Part II *Hindrances and Barriers.*)

In Mark 5, there is a story of the demon-possessed man. Jesus commanded the unclean spirit to come out of the man. It came out and Jesus permitted the demons to enter the herd of swine that were nearby. Word got around quickly for those who fed the swine fled and told it in the city and the country. Then Jesus, himself, told the man to "Go home to your friends, and tell them what great things the Lord has done for you, and how He has had compassion on you." He departed and began to proclaim in Decapolis all that Jesus had done for him, and everyone marveled.

Soon afterward, the woman with the issue of blood caught wind of the healing and the compassion of Jesus. She heard about the Man with healing power and His compassion, going around bringing hope to hurting souls. Here's a woman struggling with this unusual and debilitating sickness. All

Patricia Simon

hope was lost for she had diminished her resources and grew worse. At this juncture, she's alone with no joy and not wanting anyone to expose her private condition.

It's sad because we have many people today suffering in the same state. It might not always be physical. It could be some other adverse thing but there's a private suffering and diminished hope. This woman, after she had heard about Jesus, she purposed in her heart that she would be healed. She was desperate and bold in her pursuit.

We should pay attention! What did she have to lose even if her condition became known to the gossipers and persecutors of that day? She wanted to be healed! She set out to find the Healer. Her goal was clean and simple. "If I could just touch the hem of his garment." Her ammunition was powerful! This woman was armed with faith. She was willing to risk her reputation and freedom despite the laws. They were still under the Levitical laws of purity and cleanliness.

She believed if she could just touch the hem of His clothes she would be made well. She was right! Jesus told her, "Your faith has made you whole." This woman, with the flow of blood literally touched his clothes and was healed!

Your question might be, so how do we today touch him? We believe Jesus is the Son of God, we believe His Word, we act on His Word, and we share His Word. Acting on His Word might include everything from the laying on of hands, to using your authority, to simply resting and receiving His truths. As mentioned in my chapter on rest, rest does not mean passivity. It means that God has heard our prayer and expect that we will trust Him according to His Word which assures us that He cares for us. He leads and we trust. As we trust, we might be instructed to do something. As we move forward, we continue to uplift His name, thanking Him, offering praises, and declaring Jesus as our Lord and Savior. Prepare for the manifestation of your healing!

As Jesus, the Healer went about the land, He healed all who believed. There is nothing about this that is complex or difficult, yet it is profound. The concept is deep in its own simple way. Jesus responded favorably to those who came believing. Not everyone did. What a glorious day it will be when we begin to see more healings among believers simply because people believe in the Healer; when we begin to speak and declare healing over our bodies, and others.

One might say there are people we see today who believe and are not healed of their diseases. I don't have an answer for that. There are many variables. However, the vision here is for us to recognize and exhaust every avenue of wellness that God has provided us under the New Covenant. We have seen that believing and having faith are prerequisites to leading us in the right direction to fulfilling that vision "Beloved, I pray that you may prosper in all things and be in health, just as your soul prosper" (3 John 1:2). Let's start with believing. What we believe influences every aspect of our lives. As we begin reading the Word and building our faith, we can examine ourselves to see if there is something that hinders the manifestation of healing.

What changes need to be made in order to accommodate the promises of God? The Holy Spirit is here to comfort, lead, counsel and help us to work out hindrances and to give us the boldness to take authority over the sickness to declare our healing!

Chapter 3

The Name of Jesus

He made himself of no reputation, taking the form of a bond servant and coming in the likeness of men. and being found in appearance as a man, He humbled Himself and became obedient to the point of death, even the death of the cross. Therefore, God has also exalted him and given him the name, which is above every name, that at the name of Jesus every knee should bow, of those in heaven and of those on earth, and of those under the earth. (Philippians 2:7-10)

The writer of Hebrews tells us how God has spoken to us in these last days by His son Jesus, whom, having become so much better than the angels, as He has by inheritance obtained a more excellent name than they.

- There is power in His name and authority in His name.
- Satan knows the magnificence of this name.
- He trembles at the name of Jesus.
- Authorities cautioned Peter and John not to use this name.
- We can heal, be healed, and believe for anything in his name.
- Call on this name in any situation.

- There is forgiveness in His name.
- We find peace and joy in his name.
- We should pray in the name of Jesus.
- We should magnify and lift-up the name of Jesus.
- Have faith in his name.

In Acts 3:6, Peter tells the lame man who was lying at the gate called Beautiful and asking for charity, "Silver and gold I do not have, what I do have I give you. In the name of Jesus Christ of Nazareth, rise and walk." The man got up and walked and the people were greatly amazed for he had been crippled for eight years. Peter went on to tell the onlookers in verse 12, "Men of Israel why do you marvel at us, as though by our own power or godliness we had made this man walk?" He goes on to say in verse 16, "His name, through faith in His name has made this man strong. The faith which comes through Jesus has healed him in the presence of you all."

In Acts chapter 4, the rulers, elders, and scribes as well as the High Priest heard of the miracle and they asked Peter and John, "By what power or by what name have you done this?" Then Peter, filled with the Holy Spirit, said to them, "Rulers of the people and elders of Israel: "if we this day are judged for a good deed done to a helpless man, by what means he has been made well, let it be made known to you all, that by the name of Jesus Christ of Nazareth, whom you crucified, whom God raised from the dead, by Him this man stands before you whole. This is the stone, which was rejected by your builders, which has become the chief cornerstone. Nor is there salvation in any other for there is no other Name under heaven given among men by which we must be saved."

After the rulers, saw the healed man walking about, they recognized that a notable miracle had been done. They did not want this miracle to spread among the people. They called Peter and John and commanded them not to speak at all nor teach in the name of Jesus. Peter and John prayed for boldness to continue preaching. In Acts chapter 4:3, we're told that when they had prayed, the place where they were assembled was shaken; and they were all filled with the Holy Spirit, and they spoke the word of God with boldness.

And Jesus came and said to them, "All authority in heaven and on earth has been given to Me."

Matthew 28:18

And these signs will accompany those who believe. In My name they will cast out demons; they will speak in new tongues.

Mark 16:17

The seventy-two returned with joy saying, "Lord even the demons are subject to us in your name!"

Luke 10:17

Whatever you ask in my name, this I will do, that the Father may be glorified in the Son.

John 14:13

In that day you will ask me nothing. Most assuredly, I say to you, whatever you ask the Father In my name He will give you.

John 16:23

But when they believed Phillip as he preached the things concerning the Kingdom of God and the name of Jesus Christ, both men and women were baptized.

Acts 8:12

And whatever you do in word or deed, do all in the name of the Lord Jesus, giving thanks to God the Father through Him.

Colossians 3:17

Therefore, God has also highly exalted Him and given Him the name which is above every name. That at the name of Jesus every knee should bow, of those in heaven, and of those on earth, and of those under the earth, and that every tongue should confess that Jesus Christ is Lord, to the glory of God the Father.

Philippians 2:9-11

No matter the sickness, call on Jesus. Pray to Father in the name of Jesus. As you pray, believe for the manifestation of your healing. Remember, 1 Peter 2:24 says *by whose stripes we were healed.* Change your spiritual posture and expect a miracle because it's already done. The just shall walk by faith.

Chapter 4

The Holy Spirit and Authority

H ere are words that are lovely to our ears. In John 14:8, Jesus tells the disciples, "Although I'm going away, I will not leave you as orphans." In that day, I'm certain those words were challenging for the disciples to grasp. But for us here today, we get it! We need everything that's wrapped up in that statement, because it would be quite a feat to live without God's Holy Spirit.

It's an awesome revelation that the breath and power of God can live inside of us. For some, it's too rich a gift to believe and accept. It's akin to reconciliation, it's unfathomable! So much so that it becomes work and a struggle to invite the Holy Spirit into your tent, your temple, your body. Yes inside of you!

Some are still waiting to receive the gift of the Holy Spirit. We don't have to struggle. We just need to receive the Gift by faith. God has already sent Him to the world. We no longer need to wait. If you're having difficulty repenting of sins, or some other hindrance where the enemy is trying to convince you that you are not worthy of God's mercy, remember, none of us are! Jesus made us righteous, to receive all the blessings (spiritual and otherwise), that God has compassionately given to us. Don't be carried away into some false thinking believing God's gifts are for the *good Christians*. We may strive to be *good Christians*, but Jesus died for us when we were all yet sinners. Our righteousness is through faith in Jesus Christ to all who believe. So, repent of your sins and mean it from your heart. Acknowledge with water baptism, then ask Jesus to baptize you in the power of his Holy Spirit. In the book of Acts, starting at Chapter 2, many groups and individuals received the power of the Holy Spirit with the evidence of speaking in tongues. They were ministered to with the Word, and by the laying on of hands.

In Acts chapter 10:44, while Peter was still speaking, the Holy Spirit fell on the Gentiles. They heard Peter giving an account of how God had spoken to him to say, "Call no man common or unclean." He goes on to say, "In truth, I perceive that God shows no partiality."

We don't know whether these Gentiles were already believers. It's possible under Cornelius, they were already believing Christians because the bible tells us that Cornelius was a just man who feared God. It's also possible that they simply heard the Word that day for the first time as Peter spoke, began to believe and were filled with the Holy Spirit. The message was basically to let the Jews know that salvation had come to the Gentile world. This group at Cornelius house were baptized after they received the Holy Spirit. There's no prerequisite to receiving the Holy Spirit, other than repenting.

Water Baptism is symbolic and serves to acknowledge our new life in Jesus. We have access now. Simply repent, believe the word, and be filled. Come boldly to the throne of grace. If you prefer to have your pastor, deacon or just someone with faith, to help you with this, then do so. Make that faith connection and receive God's Holy Spirit. Receive the power!

You'll need the power to fully operate in the gifts of the spirit. You'll also want to be able to walk in the fruit of the spirit (Galatians 5:22) and partake in the five-fold ministry, (Ephesians 4:11) when the calling of God comes upon you. You need power to resist the deceiver, power to recognize familiar spirits and foolishness. We need to be equipped for ministry. All believers should be in ministry. The Holy Spirt enables us to have a more effective, power-filled experience on this journey.

This is not to say you need the Holy Spirit to be healed. I'm just emphasizing the benefits of Holy Ghost power. God wants us healed! He told us what the Comforter would do. In my own walk, I've learned to stand on God's Word. When the enemy comes against me, I'm declaring and decreeing the Word. The Holy Spirit encourages me to stand strong and to not back down in doubt and unbelief. He reminds me that the thing has already been settled in heaven and by His stripes I am healed because "Greater is He who is in me than he who is in the world" 1 John 4:4). He helps me to be vigilant in areas of deception. He helps me to have more effective prayers and times of faith-building. He helps me to have self-control. He teaches restraint.

His voice is small sometimes. Be still and listen. Even when you're at a boisterous wedding party, the Holy Spirit might whisper to say, "Careful with the sweets. The sugar in that extra piece of cake might cause you to get an earache."

You do not want my earaches, which I usually experience after too many sweets. I'm thankful for the correction and admonishment that comes from the voice of the Holy Spirit. In this book, you will hear me talk a lot about correction from God. It's beautiful to know God will take time to correct us. I think I've said this already and I'm certain you will hear it again.

Ask God to fill you, and baptize you with His Holy Spirit. If you're already filled and have been baptized in the power of the Holy Spirit, then ask God to refresh you and make you anew; to give you a fresh anointing. Don't grow stale and complacent. Stay active and vibrant. Open your heart to begin to experience signs, wonders, and a deeper revelation of God's amazing love. Receive, by faith, God's Holy Spirit in the name of Jesus! Walk in the supernatural power of God and as you receive, I pray God will bring you into a sphere of change. A place where you will witness the inner working of God's power in your life.

As we pray, we can bind sickness and disease. We have authority in the name of Jesus to rebuke, and call out sickness and infirmities, and to cast down addictions and hindrances in the body. We pray that God will send a manifestation of abundant miracles for each one of us, and our households. That He will activate a powerful healing balm as He ministers to bodies, minds, and spirits. Let's also agree, for a move of God for a fresh anointing and a supernatural ability to receive by faith and begin to walk in the boldness demonstrated in Acts 4.

Greater is He who is in me than He that is in the world (1 john 4:4). When the Holy Spirit resides in you, the devil gets nervous because now your body becomes the temple of the Holy Spirit. It's not long before you recognize the benefits of being indwelled by Him. When Jesus was raised from the dead, we were raised with Him. We are the body of Christ! Being the body here on earth, He gives us Authority. The same spirit that raised Jesus from the dead now lives in us.

Through the blood of Jesus and in His name, we can execute the same authority as Jesus did for healings and other miracles. In Mark 16:15-18, Jesus tells the disciples to preach the gospel in all the world. And he who believes and is baptized will be saved.

Verses 17 and 18 tell us of all the signs we will witness to him who believes: first, you must believe. "In my name they will cast out demons; they will speak with new tongues; they will take up serpents; and if they drink anything deadly, it will by no means hurt them; they will lay hands on the sick, and they recover." The devil does not want us to know the authority we have in Jesus' name. Rise up and declare who you are. Know your identity! Understand the power that has been given to you.

Before Jesus Himself purged our sins and went to sit at the right hand of Father, He equipped us to continue this important work. He wanted us to be ready, willing, and able to administer the teachings, being filled with power of the Holy Ghost, and exerting the authority that we have inherited as children of God. Even as He was still on earth, He wanted us to be prepared for challenging situations. Take the example at Mark 9:14-29. The disciples were having difficulty casting demons from a boy.

Jesus wanted them to know the importance of learning, growing, and maturing. This message of the Gospel would need to go from Jerusalem, Samaria, Judea and other parts of the world. It is paramount that we understand how to navigate life while imitating Jesus under the counsel of the Holy Spirit.

In the passage in Mark 9, Jesus took Peter, James, and John with him to witness the miraculous event of the

Transfiguration on the Mount. He left the other nine disciples to tend to matters at hand while He was away.

While on the mount, the disciples witnessed an extraordinary occurrence. Jesus was *transfigured* into blazing white light. He was then joined by Elijah and Moses. This experience gave the three yet another confirmation of Jesus's identity. They then heard the voice of God from heaven saying, "This is my beloved Son. Hear Him."

So it was, upon Jesus' return from this powerful experience on the Mount, that He encounters a circus of sorts. A dispute between the scribes and the disciples possibly about this demon-possessed child that the disciples could not heal. There's also a multitude running around trying to see what the confusion was all about.

The father of the child is questioning Jesus as to why the disciples were not able to heal his demon-possessed son. Lastly, we have bewildered disciples who were also wondering why they'd failed in this deliverance process. After all, they'd been taught by Jesus.

As the father approached Jesus with all this confusion in the background, he said, "Teacher, I brought you my son, who has a mute spirit. And whenever it seizes him, it throws him down, he foams at the mouth and so forth. I spoke to your disciples, but they could not help me." The father evidently had believing issues much like the others.

Jesus answers and says, "O faithless generation, how long shall I be with you? How long shall I bear with you? Bring him to me" (Mark 9:14-29). Jesus tells the father of the child, "If you can believe, all things are possible to him who believes." The man cried out, "Lord I believe, help my unbelief."

Jesus called the spirit out of the child, and he was healed. The main point is that Jesus wants us to be well-equipped to do this work and He also wants onlookers to experience this demonstration of God's power! In the end of the thing, the disciples asked Jesus, "Why were we not able to heal the boy?" Jesus tells them, this kind can only come out by prayer and fasting.

"Put on the whole armor of God that you may be able to stand against the wiles of the devil" (Ephesians 6:11). That means that we should know what our spiritual resources are. What weaponry do we employ when faced with the enemy's attacks as this father and child were? Ephesians 6:12 tells us we do not wrestle against flesh and blood but against principalities, against powers, against the rulers of the darkness of this age, against spiritual hosts of wickedness in the heavenly places. It goes on to tell us to take up the whole armor of God, that you may be able to withstand in the evil day.

To withstand and be prepared for spiritual warfare, you're told to:

Gird your waist with the belt of truth (know the truth of God's Word). Believe it, act on it, rest in it, defend it, and guard it, keeping it close to your heart! His Words are medicine, protection, provision, direction for any and all issues of life. Settle these truths in your spirit person. This will equip you for life.

Keep yourself girded up with the truth so that when the enemy strikes, you'll be ready for battle. When you get bludgeoned with lying symptoms, or whispers of defeat, remind the devil who lives inside of you (1 John 4:4). Gear-up with this belt by proclaiming that God's Word is true and this truth enables you to exude confidence that reminds others that you not only trust in the truth of God's Word, but you live it.

Put on the breastplate of righteousness. Conduct yourselves according to the Word. Keep an obedient heart. Wear compassion as a reminder of what Christ has done for you and therefore remember the need to love others. You are righteous because He has made you righteous. Let your light shine so that others may see your good works and glorify your Father in heaven (Matthew 5:16). Be a watchman over your heart and guard it diligently. Walk in the light, honoring God with humility and holiness (1 Peter1:15, 16).

Shod your feet with the gospel of peace. Share the good news in love and peace encouraging others to be reconciled to God (1 Corinthians 5:20). Declare His Word. Share your excitement with others! Have compassion for souls so that you might win some for the kingdom. The last thing demons want is for you to share the good news. Share, share and share some more. Heaven rejoices when you tell others, and souls are turned to God. This is a mighty defense mechanism, though you might not perceive it as such (Luke 15:7-10).

Take the shield of faith. Believe and trust God and His Word. Believing is the key (Mark 9:23). Hold up the banner of faith especially in situations that appear to be impossible. When all else fails and the snake is pounding you with lies and thoughts of giving up, continue in faith. The righteous shall live by faith. When the enemy sends his fiery darts, it's your faith in God's promises that will sustain you (Romans 1:17).

Take the helmet of salvation. On this road you have to guard your mind against ungodly thoughts and temptations. The wicked one will set traps. But as you endeavor to stay in the race, despite the opposition, take hold of the spiritual weaponry and defend your inheritance. Embrace hope and the promise of eternal life not yielding to the adversary's voice while continuing to share your hope with others. Lift up the name of Jesus and keep your eyes on Him. The helmet enables you to maintain vigilance and be in position to resist the wicked one. You rest in full assurance that victory has already been won, and that faith and hope will carry you to your eternal dwelling (John 3:13, 14).

Take the sword of the Spirit which is the Word of God. As you suit up with the other armor, the sword is the weapon that will enable you to respond offensively. Read the word, hear the word, live the word, love the word, protect the word and wield the Word. There are powerful healing Scriptures you can decree. Speak the Word in faith to bring alive God's promises in your life. The enemy strives to defeat you and to steal the Word from your heart. Fight back with the Word of God, just as Jesus did during the time of his forty-day fast when Satan appeared to him with words of temptation (Matthew 4:1-11). The same can be done by speaking over our sickness. Also remember, that Jesus is the Word and will fight for you according to His promises. We're covered at all angles.

Praying with power. Start now, proclaiming the truth of God's Word, taking authority over adversities as you have authority in Jesus name. Rebuke sickness, financial hindrances, job concerns, or relational situations. As mentioned, Jesus didn't leave us as orphans. He sent us a Helper. Be filled with the Spirit of God! Ask Him to pour out His Spirit upon you and baptize you with the Holy Spirit and fire. so that the indwelling will give you the power and authority you need to pray for you and your loved ones. Speak in tongues or use your prayer language as the Holy Spirit enables you.

Remember Elijah? In James 5, it explains that the effective, fervent prayer of a righteous man avails much. It goes on to say, that Elijah was a man with a nature like ours, and he prayed earnestly that it would not rain; and it did not rain on the land for three years and six months. He prayed again, and the heavens gave rain.

Speak out in boldness like Peter did in Lydda: "Jesus, the Christ, heals you! Arise and make your bed. Aeneas, who was paralyzed and had been bedridden for eight years, arose immediately" (Acts 9:32).

Remember Paul at Philippi and the girl possessed with the spirit of divination. The girl followed Paul crying out about the *men of God*. The Bible tells us that she did this for many days, and Paul was greatly annoyed. At last, he said to the spirit, "I command you in the name of Jesus Christ to come out of her." It came out that very hour (Acts 16:16-24).

Acts 19:11,12 tells that God worked unusual miracles by the hand of Paul. Each Jesus-follower can call on God by whatever means available. His will is for every believer to be well. You can command the thing or pray and petition God while laying on hands for healing. Employ all Bible resources and promises. It's already been done! Receive it by faith. Rebuke, cast out, bind, and believe. Whichever method you employ, faith and believing are necessary. You must believe! You will effectively walk in the promises of God through the believing of His Word. Activate your faith and see the miracles. As mentioned earlier, there might be hindrances. Still, move in faith and let the Holy Spirit reveal to you how to receive your healing, or whatever you are seeking God for. Grow and begin to develop your faith. Faith comes by hearing the Word of God (Romans 10:17).

Hebrews 6:13,14 tells us that everyone who partakes only of milk is unskilled in the word of righteousness, for he is a babe. But solid food belongs to those who are of full age, those who by reason of use have their senses exercised to discern both good and evil.

It's time to move on to greater heights by putting God's Word into action. Let's not neglect the meatier things, rendering useless the power God has given. This is not to say one must have a thorough knowledge of the Word before experiencing healing or other miracles. However, every Christian should know the promises of God to rightly partake of them and begin to declare them. No one can live off another person's faith. It's important to grow and know how to call on God and to get in His presence.

In 1 Samuel 30:6, we're told how King David, after discovering that his city of Ziklag was burned down and his family and those of his followers had been taken captive, that David strengthened himself in the Lord his God.

He put on his priestly garments before inquiring to the Lord about what to do. The Lord answered David, and all was restored. We must be able to get in the presence of God and, like David, inquire what to do about any situation plaguing us or the people around us.

You might say, "David was a King and was in position to do more than I can." Under the New Covenant we have better promises. We are sons and daughters and priests. Because of the Holy Spirit living inside us we can go before God the same way as the Patriarchs, whether it be for healing, salvation for loved ones, or whatever the need.

God is Holy! Live right, obey His Word. Get into His presence with praise and thanksgiving! Talk to God. Then, be still! Listen to Holy Spirit. Let the Holy Spirit remind you of your authority and how to move forward from life's challenges and struggles. If you're concerned about spiritual development and ministries, God has a plan to help you work it out.

There will always be different kinds of adversities hovering about, but with prayer, worship, and armor (David was geared up), it lessens the fear and confrontation. Subsequently, you can move past the obstacle, giving God the glory.

You might ask, "What does it mean to be geared up?" Remember your armor described in Ephesians 6, and simply live your best life according to God's Word. Don't wait to gear up. Stay geared up! Stay in God's presence. Continue worshipping Him. Worship is an attitude. Let everything you do reflect worship and reverence to God. Stay vigilant and keep your eyes on Jesus.

I mentioned earlier about eating cakes and sweets. I've always suffered with severe ear pain. It was not known to me nor the medical community the reason for the ear pain. I started noticing my ear aching when eating too many sweets. After suffering for years, I began to monitor my sugar intake, and then realized sugar was the culprit.

After much prayer, struggle, suffering, and binding and loosing, the Holy Spirit helped me to gage my sugar intake, to know my threshold and to be aware of added sugar in food products (Matthew 16:19). Once I began to yield, listen, and obey, I found the strength and discipline I needed to keep the earaches at bay. While I'm not wholly healed of the earaches, I thank God that in this process of cautioning me, He has help me to engage in healthy eating. I feel much better as I limit my sugar.

Isn't that just like God? I wasn't disciplined enough to do this on my own. I needed help. God will allow certain adverse situations for correctional purposes. It's all for the good, though. There are times when I still try to overindulge. His small voice will remind me. Hours later I will feel the tingling of ear pain that would have worsened had I not obeyed. "Thank you, Jesus, for helping us in our weakness."

Maybe you have an illness of this nature that causes you to be sick. Let Holy Spirit minister to you to help you work it out. Sure, I could take the anti-inflammatory medicine that the doctor tried to give me. It probably would have eased my pain, but it would not have solved the problem. I probably would have continued to indulge in bad eating habits, because certain medicines—such as blood pressure pills—enable poor eating habits.

I once asked a group of people sitting around a table filled with unhealthy food, how many were taking blood pressure medicine. Most of them were. The attitude was, "The medicine will cover the sodium, even though I hate taking it."

God wants us well. If He made us well at the Cross, we need to start honoring Him rather than taking our blessings for granted. Let the Holy Spirit help you get to the root cause of your illness. He will give you the strength to make the necessary adjustment.

Medicine might help but don't let the medicine rob you of an opportunity to believe God for your healing. Medicine is spiritually and physically weighty, expensive, and in many cases causes side effects. It's spiritually weighty because people abhor the idea of taking medicine. It's bothersome and goes against what we know and understand. Of course, there are many situations where medicine is of great help. Still, it gnaws at our spirit to take it.

Proverbs 4:20-23 tells us that God's Word is health to your flesh. Start believing God's Word and by faith, receive your healing! Oftentimes, healing is not the issue. The problem could be that we need to use wisdom to find the needed relief.

The account of the woman with an issue of blood was referred to earlier (Mark 5:25-35). She heard about Jesus and decided, "If I can touch his clothes, I will be made whole." Faith comes by hearing the Word or reading the Word. She established her faith. She decided in her heart that she needed to touch Him. When the time came for her to touch His garment, she was made well. The Bible tells us she had spent all she had going to doctors, but grew worse.

Go to the doctor when you need to, but have your heart fixed on Jesus. Set your mind on divine healing. It draws you closer to God. It draws others to God and opens doors for other miracles because you become zealous for the things of God.

There might be other avenues for your healing but as mentioned, give Jesus a chance. Don't let fear deny you the experience that is expressed and demonstrated in God's healing love for you. Depend on Jesus! Don't wait till you go broke, or your condition worsens. Our initial response to a medical diagnosis should be to call on our Healer, our Deliverer. That's not always easy! Depending on the diagnosis, fear can set in and confuse your thinking.

Call yourself healed! Call out to God! Declare His promises! Lay hands on the part of your body affecting you.

Pray this prayer:

Lord, Your Word tells us that that You bore our sickness on the Cross and by Your stripes we were healed. If You be for me, who can be against me, Lord. Greater is He who is in me than He who is in the world. Your Holy Spirit lives in me, Lord. The enemy has no claim on this body, for this body is the temple of Your Holy Spirit. You said, when we believe, all things are possible. You said, when we believe we will see Your glory (the manifest presence of Your power). Thank You for Your lovingkindness and thank You for sending Jesus that we might be healed.

(Matthew 8:18; Romans 8:31; 1 John 4:4; 1 Corinthians 6:19; Mark 9:23; John 11:40)

Lose the pride and humble yourself before God and man to act on His Word. Sometimes there must be indignation as shown by blind Bartimaeus. Bartimaeus didn't care who was offended by his cries for help. He needed Jesus! He wanted to see! He was willing to give up whatever aid he was receiving. He wanted to throw off the tunic that labeled him as a blind citizen, who was thought to be unfit to speak in the public square (Mark 10:46-52).

Lift your hands and call on Jesus. Worship and praise God in the assembly. Don't just sit there composed and yet in need of a miracle. Throw off that tunic; that thing that's keeping you from being receptive to the holy power of God, that thing that's keeping you from recciving. Throw it off! Get rid of the doubt, fear, and concern of what others might think.

Get rid of the sugar, salty snacks, and fried foods that are keeping you unhealthy. You might say, "I know this caffeine is not good for me, but I need my cup of coffee in the morning." Get rid of the drinking and smoking that could hinder your healing.

Next, get rid of the lying, cheating, and hating. Let go of the unforgiveness that you may have been justifying.

Some people don't care to take control of these things. They may say, "I'll die before I talk to them again." Or, "They'll never get an apology from me, I'll die first." Oftentimes, they do.

All this hinders your identity in Jesus and the devil plays on it. He recognizes that you have no authority because you are still functioning under his government—under the curse. Galatians 3:13,14 tells us that Jesus has redeemed us from the curse of the law, having become the curse for us, for it is written, "Cursed is anyone who hangs on a tree."

If someone has wronged you, remember that Jesus said, "Bless those who curse you, and pray for those who spitefully use you (Luke 6:28). Don't fall back under Satan's dominion. Under the law, we had no recourse other than annual atonement for our sins through the high priest. Today, we're under a new covenant with better promises. So, if someone distresses you, forgive them. If you distress them, ask for forgiveness. Don't hold it in your heart. Ephesians 9:27 tell us not to give place to the devil.

When we hold it, that's exactly what we do. We give Satan an open invitation to come into our lives and bring chaos. Then we become sick from the ordeal, either from holding animosity in our bones, or from Satan himself, for we know he comes to steal, kill and destroy. Let's wake up and rebuke the evil that plagues us which, oftentimes, we permit because we lose our identity in Christ.

Let the devil know that you know who you are. That you know your rights. You know your authority. You are a son or daughter of the Most High. An heir to the Kingdom of God. A member of the body of Christ. The Holy Ghost lives in you and the devil can have no part of you.

We want our prayers answered. We want no interference from the devil. Exercise your authority and know that as a believer, you have full assurance of sonship and inheritance. With sonship comes privileges, benefits, and the authority to speak for yourself and for others when you believe. Get your healing today, in the name of Jesus!

Chapter 5

Where Did Sickness Come From?

> *Then the Lord God took the man and put him in the Garden of Eden to tend to it and keep it. And the Lord commanded the man, saying, "Of every tree of the garden you may freely eat, but of the tree of the knowledge of good and evil you shall not eat, for in that day you eat of it you shall surely die."*
>
> Genesis 2:15-17

In the above passage, the Lord gives a clear admonition to Adam. However, in Genesis 3, we see that Satan plants doubt in the mind of Eve. "Has God indeed said, you shall not eat of every tree of the garden?" (Genesis 3:1)

The dynamics of this exchange between the serpent and Eve was derived from a web of embellished deceptions on the part of Satan. This exchange, Satan's ploy, culminated into straight up disobedience for Eve and spilled over to Adam. Adam and Eve did not physically immediately die, but did so spiritually.

Disobedience in the garden, formed a different course for mankind; a gradual path leading to ailments, fear, and death.

Romans 5:12 says, "Therefore, just as through one man sin entered the world, and death through sin, and thus death spread to all men, because all sinned."

As Eve conversed with the serpent, we witness the spirit of doubt and conflict transpiring. Then, we see desire and temptation coming to the forefront. Doubt, desire, and temptation are not bad in their proper place, but when it involves communal defiance resulting in relational jeopardy, then the structured economy is affected. As we read the early account, we also see fear, accusation, and guilt taking shape and becoming a part of man's progressive decline. These are all common traits that contribute to sickness and poor health. As Adam and Eve ignored God's warning not to partake of the tree of knowledge of good and evil, their authority was stripped from them, and Satan became the god of the air.

Unknowingly, Adam and Eve surrendered their rights as overseers of the earth and handed all authority to Satan.

Do you not know that to whom you present yourselves to obey, you are that one's slaves to obey, whether of sin leading to death or of obedience leading to righteousness.

Romans 6:16

Because the trajectory was now death, sickness was inevitable. Since the Mosaic law had not been instituted, sin and death loomed heavily over the earth. Remember though, the law of Moses was a temporary system until propitiation occurred following the death and resurrection of Jesus.

After their fall from God's economy in the Garden of Eden, Adam and Eve were sent out of the garden. Otherwise, they would have lived forever in sin, eating from the tree of life, knowing good and evil with no hope of salvation. But God set man's course with the redemptive promise of Genesis 3:15. Father had a plan. For that plan to be effective our first family had to leave the garden. The disease of sin had crept its way into man's existence.

The trauma of exiting the garden, leaving the abundant life, had to have been devastating. Now faced with an unknown culture of survival, threats and anxiety, Adam and Eve had to find their way. Despite their disobedience, God provided coverings for them to hide their nakedness. A reminder of God's love and compassion for us even during our times of weakness and error.

As they journeyed out from God's eternal, peaceful presence of wellness and provision, they stumbled onto a ruthless reality laced with child-bearing pains, sibling rivalry leading to murder, sweat of the brow from toiling in the fields, and a seemingly diminishing hope of ever having an Eden-like experience outside of the garden. Here lies a rip in the fabric of mankind's landscape. A tear that would alter the path of the human condition and would facilitate chaos and the deterioration of man's physical, mental, emotional, and spiritual being. But God had a plan.

Under this new environment, stress is imminent. Once worry and anxiety sets in, our bodies begin to break down. We stop eating healthy, we experience relational issues, and physical and mental adversity. Satan used their son Cain to murder his brother Abel. This act had to have inflicted immeasurable damage—mentally and physically—on our first parents.

The serpent saw Abel's ability to activate the Genesis 3:15 plan of redemption simply by his act of worship through his offerings. Satan couldn't stand the idea that someone was worshipping God. He trembled at the thought of having his head crushed by the Seed. He would continue to deceive and use whomever he could, to halt God's plan of restoration and reconciliation, starting with the death of Abel. Sickness and death prevailed, courtesy of the serpent. He was now the prince of the air. This gave him authority and a legal right to cause trouble. John 10:10 tells us, the thief comes only to steal, kill, and destroy.

After Cain killed Abel, the worldly Cain nation had arrived and was recognized on the world's stage. Cain, more than likely, married a cousin of Adam and Eve's other children because they had more children. Cain's innovations and various progressive industries, including music, bronze, cattle and again, murder, set their standards for living large. Their boom on the scene was such a rumble that the godly Seth nation took notice.

Seth was another son of Adam and Eve. The Seth nation consisted of people of God. The Bible tells us that after Seth was born, people began to call on the name of God. The men of Seth paid attention to the lovely women of Cain and began to intermarry. This was yet another of Satan's attempt to thwart God's plan. Satan's plan was to take God's holy nation (the people who were serving God at that time) and pollute them with the evil Cain society in order to diminish or quash the future fulfillment of Israel (though Israel had not yet been named), bringing forth the seed, Jesus.

At this stage, the earth and its inhabitants had become inherently evil. The serpent had succeeded in this part of his plan to win over the people of God for his purpose. At first, God's righteous ones served Him and lived in obedience, until they were enticed by the loose living of Cain's people. They had no legal standards and no mediator. But they knew right from wrong.

Today, we have the Word of God as our standard, we have the Holy Spirit as our Teacher and Guide, we have a Redeemer who is our Mediator. We have no excuse for evil.

> *Be sober, be vigilant for your adversary the devil walks about like a roaring lion, seeking whom he may devour…*
>
> 1 Peter 5:8

Though Seth's generation had called on the name of God, and set their ways as righteous, they were still lured by the lust of the flesh into ungodly territory; again, at the courtesy of Satan. God's creation had plunged into the depths of sin and wicked living which produces sickness in the bones, in the mind, and in the soul. As stated in Genesis 6, it would be 120 years before God would put an end to the chaos.

> *And the LORD said, "My Spirit shall not strive with man forever, for he is indeed flesh; yet his days shall be one hundred and twenty years."*
>
> Genesis 6:3

The Cain generation, coupled with the Seth descendants, had produced great men of renown; mighty men, who were arrogant, ungodly, and wicked. The Lord saw that the wickedness of man was great. At this stage, there was only one righteous, and that was Noah. God will always make a way for his people. He will always help you to see the truth to receive your healing. There's no obstacle so big or difficult that God can't help you.

As God destroyed the world by water, Noah and his family found refuge in the ark that God instructed Noah to build. When all was said and done, and the new world began to take shape with Noah and his family, we see in Scripture that Satan once again crept into man's reality with a determined plan of action to destroy God's people. The agent of sickness and disease had spilled over into the Postdiluvian Era—the days following Noah's flood. Though God's plan of salvation was still forthcoming, Satan yet continued his plotting before and after the flood.

There were two separate times when Abraham and Sarah pretended to be sister and brother (they were husband and wife, having the same father but not the same mother) when Pharaoh and Abimelech had eyes on Sarah. These unauthorized relationships would have tainted the seed.

During the time of Moses, murder attempts were made on babies of the children of Israel to limit the male children.

There were various battles where evil leaders tried to destroy Israel.

Haman under King Ahasuerus and Queen Esther, tried to slaughter the Jews,

Plus, many other countless accounts where Satan attempted to bring death and destruction or pollute the seed. Of course, during these times, sickness, sin and death continued.

When Jesus died on the cross, He absorbed it all. Sin, shame, guilt, sickness, hurt, pain, horror, poverty, sorrow, emotional trauma—whatever the issue, it was laid upon Jesus. He took a beating for any imaginable harm that had plagued mankind since Satan began wielding his evil plans. He took away our troubles and our sins in exchange for grace.

It's easier for us to accept that He took away our sins, than it is to accept that he also took away our hurt. Our reasonable response should be to receive these promises by faith, and by offering thanksgiving and honor. Ironically though, we still hurt. Oftentimes this is because we continue to engage in behavior that opens the door to Satan's attacks. These behaviors may include disobedience, eating unhealthy foods, overeating, or being irresponsible with finances (poor stewards). Might we be dishonoring God's redemptive blessings by engaging in behavior that counteracts His gifts and benefits?

If we recognize that we were healed by Jesus at the cross, our behavior should reflect that. We would eat foods that contribute to whole health in order to honor the blessing. We must put our belief into action. Our Heavenly Father did not want His children to suffer any longer, so He executed a plan to liberate us.

Confess Jesus as Lord, embrace redemption by faith and rest in the promises of God's Word. Honor God's plan of redemption and the hope of salvation by walking in obedience and being vigilant of the enemy's continued attempt to draw us away from God. Again, resist the devil and he will flee.

Observe the transformation taking place in your life and know that you already have everything you need to live a godly, healthy, and peaceful life. It doesn't stop there. You must still intercede for others. Pray and seek wellbeing for others according to God's Word.

Thank you, Jesus, for helping us to grow and to share your love with others.

Chapter 6

Prayer, Fasting, And Order

A s believers in Jesus, expressing our faith is the key to spiritual growth and development. There are various ways to demonstrate our beliefs. The most common is prayer. As we read the Word of God and our eyes are spiritually opened, we understand that praying is our lifeline. Prayer is our faith connection, not only to build us up but to express adoration as we come before Father in honor, praise, worship, and thanksgiving. Of course, these should be a part of our normal everyday attitudes as we have communion with God.

Adoration before God is pivotal to our personal and spiritual walk.

- Thanksgiving brings great joy to our soul.
- Honoring God keeps us humble.
- Continuous praise gives us a peaceful countenance.
- Worship helps us to maintain a posture of reverence.

Not rigid or by works, but a natural and fitting response of love. After King David brought the Ark of the Covenant to Mt. Zion, he acquired musical instruments for the tabernacle. He instituted a 24-hour system of praise, worship, and adoration to God with Levites, singers, and musicians to minister before the ark. He spent time lavishing adoration and praise in God's presence. David knew God, and he understood how to have intimacy with God through praise and worship. Look at how God responds to David at the end of Psalm 91

> *Because he has set his love upon Me, Therefore, I will deliver him. I will set him on high, because he has known My name. He shall call upon Me, and I will answer him.*
>
> Psalm 91:14, 15

Adopting these attitudes toward our Father, richly enhances our journey. It lends more depth to the time we spend in prayer and encourages us to be more disciplined in carving time out for communion with God. When we have a heart filled with adoration toward God, it makes our time of petitioning, interceding, or worshipping, much more gratifying and peaceful. Peaceful because whether we receive an immediate answer to our prayer or not, we are strengthened and have full assurance knowing that God will work it out. We can rest in His Word, declaring total provision, including healing and any other request. Thank you, Jesus!

Through prayer, we can seek such things as wisdom, forgiveness, protection, provision, and purpose. My own personal prayer times include a great deal of praise, thanksgiving, and simply worshipping God. Intercessory prayer is vital too. It's important to pray for others not only for physical and material needs, but for salvation. Many don't know how to pray for themselves. The Bible tells us that the Holy Spirit helps us in the area of prayer (Romans 8:26). Let the Holy Spirit give you wisdom and insight when praying for others. Don't be quick to give up in your prayer time. Seek God to find answers to your prayers, and for others.

There are many different types of prayers. Most will fall in the area of petition or command. Petition is simply making a request to God.

Prayer of Petition

Daniel 9:16-19 is a good example of a prayer of petition and intercession where Daniel is praying to God on behalf of Israel and asking for forgiveness of sins. Although Israel was in captivity at the time, Daniel still saw the need to petition God and ask for forgiveness of the sins that had brought them in the hands of Babylon's fury.

Here we see that we can pray and ask God for any concerns because communion with God, along with the reading of His Word, helps to develop fellowship and intimacy with Him even during times of correction. This is when we might be experiencing chastisement as a result of disobedience.

Though we have forgiveness with God under the new and living way (John 14:6), we still need to come before God during times of disobedience and ask for forgiveness of sins. Out of the sacrifice that was made for us, we should have a contrite heart that says, "Father, I'm sorry, please forgive me."

In general, talk to God about any needs, including healing. Appreciate and honor Him for what has already been done. The way we live our lives should be a clear portrayal of thanksgiving and gratefulness. Salvation is free. Wisdom, knowledge, understanding, and the fruit of the spirit are acquired marks of the Holy Spirit. The Holy Spirit will teach and lead in how to pray, and to live a life reflecting thanksgiving and praise for the tender mercies of God.

Prayer of Command/Authority

On the other hand, the prayer of command is speaking over a matter or speaking to a thing or person. It might be an opposing force, or proclaiming life, healing, deliverance and/or restoration over a situation. Jesus employed this type for most of His healings. He spoke directly to the person or demon. We also note Peter and Paul engaging in the prayer of command after Christ's ascension. Peter in Acts 3:6, at the Beautiful Gate called to the crippled man to rise and walk in the Name of Jesus.

Later, in Acts 14:8, Paul, observing a crippled man and seeing that he had the faith to be healed, said with a loud voice, "Stand up straight on your feet!" And the man leaped and walked. The people at Lystra were so amazed that they thought Paul and Barnabas were gods.

The point is, through the power of the Holy Spirit we can speak directly to the situations or petition God for our needs. Earlier we discussed taking authority which tends to fall under prayer of command. This approach is highly effective in situations of healing.

Fasting

Queen Esther called for a fast in order to help save her people from the wicked Haman. The king of Nineveh also called for a fast to save the Ninevites from the wrath of God during the time of Jonah. The prophet Daniel fasted and prayed when he realized that it was Israel's sinful nature that sparked the 70-year captivity judgement. There are many examples in the Old and New Testaments where fasting was a part of normal existence.

- Scripture tells us in Daniel 1, that Daniel fasted at the start of Judah's captivity eating only bread and vegetables for ten days in order to pay homage to his God while serving under King Nebuchadnezzar's reign. He declined the king's fancy food to reveal how the God of Israel would keep him and his friends as strong as those who were eating the King's food.

- Daniel prayed and fasted in Daniel 9:3 as he prayed for his people.

- Daniel's other fast in Daniel 10:2, reflects a period of mourning for three weeks where Daniel was disturbed concerning a message he'd received about Israel being dominated by gentile nations for years to come. Daniel understood the message even though it was a long time ahead before the events of the message would unfold. It was then that Daniel fasted, for he was mourning Israel's fate. Scripture tells us Daniel ate no pleasant food, wine, or meat for 21 days. On the third day after Daniel's 21-day fast, Daniel had a great vision of a glorious man or Angel of the Lord. Daniel was told in great detail of the events that would take place concerning Israel.

- When Nehemiah heard about the walls of Jerusalem were down, he fasted and prayed while mourning. In Nehemiah 9, he also offers a great prayer of confession and worship after the walls were erected.

- In 2 Samuel 12, David fasted and prayed for the life of his child. The Bible tells us, though the Lord put away his sin, the child died. David arose from the ground, washed, anointed himself, changed his clothes, and went into the house of the Lord and worshipped.

- In Matthew 4:1-3, Jesus fasted forty days in the wilderness

- In Luke 2:36-38, Anna the prophetess bore witness to Jesus. The Bible tells us that she never left the temple but stayed fasting and praying day and night.

- In Matthew 6:16-18, Jesus discusses how fasting is to be seen only by God.
- In Matthew 17:14-21, Jesus tells His disciples to fast and pray.
- In Acts 13:1-3, the church at Antioch fasted and prayed and laid hands on Paul and Barnabas as they sent them out.
- In Acts 14:21-23 it tells us that Paul and Barnabas prayed and fasted in every church

We fast when we're seeking God for answers to a particular situation. We abstain from food while looking to God to help us in our time of bewilderment or for spiritual growth. Fasting equips us to engage in deeper communion and heightened intimacy with God.

Jesus taught on healing in the area of deliverance from demons. (Matthew 17:14-21) The disciples wanted to know why they were not successful in healing the sick and demon possessed child. Jesus said, in this case, to believe, fast, and pray. Also, in Matthew He said *when* you fast, not *if* you fast. Fasting was expected as part of basic principles.

The prophet Isaiah instructs us on the type of fasting that is pleasing to God and the fasting that is not pleasing (Isaiah 58). Fasting that pleases God:

- To lose the bonds of wickedness
- To undue the heavy burdens
- To let the oppressed, go free.
- To break every yoke
- To share your bread with the hungry
- Bring to your house the poor who are cast out.
- When you see the naked that you cover him and not hide yourself from your own flesh. (don't neglect or reject others needing help, especially those of your own family).

Scripture tells us,

> *Then your light shall break forth like the morning, your healing shall spring forth speedily, And your righteousness shall go before you; The glory of the LORD shall be your rear guard. Then you shall call, and the Lord will answer; You shall cry, and He will say, "Here I am."*
>
> Isaiah 58:8,9

Fasting does not please God if we make our voices heard on high, or to draw attention to ourselves so that others might see that we are fasting. When we spend time in earnest prayer and fasting before God, we gain a better understanding concerning an infirmity and possible steps to take for breakthrough.

Order

Though we're New Testament believers living under grace, oftentimes, when we hear words in the church pertaining to order, such as arrangement or disposition of people or things, we may think it's legalism. The Isaiah Scripture in the past section concerning fasting is relevant today. There is order in God's Kingdom. Whether we're seeking a healing or have some other request, we still must abide by God's instructions and His government.

In our marriage, family, church, our jobs, our community, our nation, and throughout the earth, there are Kingdom principles governing the order of things concerning life on earth. Order is necessary for God's people to thrive and to effectively win souls. There may be times when we are out of order, believing that anything goes under our New Testament covenant of grace.

When marriages are out of order, the children suffer. When there's no honor and respect in the household, the entire family is in chaos and needs healing. The husband and wife must present themselves in prayer, unity, sincerity, and honor before God and the family, that the children might respond favorably. This is sometimes difficult because children will oftentimes have outside influences. Prayer, unity, and wisdom from the Holy Spirit is essential. We must also abide by the guidelines set forth at our jobs, in our communities, and our country.

The same goes for our church and our spiritual life. The spirit of offense is prevalent in churches and the enemy uses this tactic to bring much hurt and confusion to many relationships. The root cause is often insecurity (a stronghold), which leads to demonic disruptions and division which cunningly arrives on the scene tearing apart groups and relationships.

Many times, the issue at hand is trivial but when emotions flare, hurt and division is eminent. This is a sad event that grips many places of worship. Anger has so engulfed the parties involved that it often severs relationships with each other and with God. Even when people feel their relationship with God has not been affected, we still need to find a way to reconcile differences so that the heart remains humble before man and God. Otherwise, bitterness will fill the space in hearts and hinder intimacy with God.

Though Jesus brought us freedom, He demonstrated order for our spiritual walk. The Apostle Paul gives us many examples of what it means to have order in church, and still live our lives in the freedom that Jesus has granted. We know Jesus redeemed us from the curse of the law (Galatians 3:10-

14). What does that mean? He took the curse upon Himself as He bought us from the slavery of sin which came upon us from our first parents. The Bible tells us that Christ became the curse for us when He hung there on a tree, because cursed is anyone who hangs on a tree.

We're not in bondage, nor burdened with cumbersome laws, because we are justified by faith. We have freedom to worship and share our beliefs, but in many parts of the world, the freedom to share the gospel is either life threatening or nonexistent. However, the freedom of the finished work of Jesus is still recognized and appreciated. What does this freedom mean?

We have freedom to serve God in obedience and truth. We have the freedom to read His Holy Word, and we have access to the throne of glory by way of the shed blood of Jesus. With access, we can petition God and make requests. We are privileged to be filled with His holy power, and free to resist the evil one. We are free to make choices.

What then determines how we make choices under the New Covenant? Are we free to do whatever? Are there parameters to our Christian liberties? Let's see what, Scripture has to say.

All things are lawful for me, but not all things are helpful; all things are lawful for me, but not all things edify.

1 Corinthians 10:23

This passage specifically refers to idolatry and idol offerings. Though in a general sense, Paul is reminding the Corinthians to do all things to the glory of God.

Paul then adds this:

> *Let no one seek his own, but each one the other's well-being.*
>
> 1 Corinthians 10:24

It appears that Paul is encouraging the believers to use discernment before making choices, and to not let our choices become a stumbling block to someone who has not spiritually matured in the understanding of Christian liberties.

> *For though I am free from all men, I have made myself a servant to all, that I might win the more...*
>
> 1 Corinthians 9:19

He was making the point that we should consider our conduct so that we might win a soul in the process.

When speaking to the Galatians concerning circumcision, Paul stated, "Stand fast therefore in the liberties by which Christ has made us free, and do not be entangled again with a yoke of bondage" (Galatians 5:1,2). He meant there was no need to go under the law. Circumcision was not needed.

He then added, "For you brethren, have been called to liberty; only do not use liberty as an opportunity for the flesh, but through love serve one another" (Galatians 5:13).

When speaking to Jewish believers who were having difficulties amid persecution, Peter said, "For this is the will of God, that by doing good you may put to silence the ignorance of foolish men. Yet, not using your liberty as a cloak for vice, but as bondservants of God." He went on to say, "Honor all people, love the brotherhood. Fear God. Honor the King" (1 Peter 2:15-17).

Jesus' prescription for order is to, "Love God and love each other" (Mark 12:30,31). The New Testament covenant bears grace-related commands and regulations that we, as believers, must adhere to in order to fully thrive under the blessings He has given us. God has equipped us to be able to walk according to the spirit and not the flesh, so that we may abide in Him as His Word abides in us. With this in mind we recognize we are debtors, not to the flesh, to live according to the flesh but to live in the spirit. For as many as are led by the spirit of God, these are sons of God. The Spirit Himself bears witness with our spirit that we are children of God (Romans 8:12-16).

God established order in the beginning. Under the Old Testament, the Mosaic laws were given to tutor God's people in preparation for Messiah. There were sacrificial and ceremonial laws, civic laws, and God's moral laws, (the Ten Commandments) supposedly, 613 laws total. Though we're not subject to the Mosaic laws, we still need to reverence and honor God and know His character which is represented in the moral commands.

Today, we see the order and character of God as we read the Old and New Testaments. We have read how God warned the Israelites concerning fasting in the book of Isaiah. We see order and instructions also in the following.

The Old Testament
- Creation
- Garden of Eden—to bless and establish economy for God's creation.
- The building of Noah's Ark—to save and start afresh.
- Moses and the ten plagues—bring God's people out of Egypt.

- Instructions for collecting the manna that fell from heaven—to feed the children of Israel in the wilderness, to reinforce Sabbath rules, and to set forth discipline.
- The design and functions of the tabernacle, the priests' duties, and the priests' attire were to establish a system of worship, order, and atonement.
- Sacrificial laws, civic laws, and the moral laws—representing how man would be in relationship with God under the law.
- The 40-year wilderness started out as an 11-day journey gone awry due to disobedience.
- Exiting the wilderness, entering Jericho, dividing the land, instructions for entering Canaan
- Abraham, Sarah and Isaac, the son of promise
- The twelve tribes, the 70-year captivity, the prophets
- The rebuilding of the Temple
- Malachi's message of judgement and hope

The New Testament
- John the Baptist and the ordinance of water baptism
- Instructions to Mary, Joseph, Elizabeth, and Zachariah in preparation for the birth of Jesus
- The birth of Jesus, the wise men, the selection of the twelve disciples
- Sermon on the mount, the miracles, the Olivet discourse
- The ordinance of communion
- The arrest, the Crucifixion, resurrection and ascension of Jesus
- Selecting another disciple to replace Judas.
- Pentecost (receiving the Holy Spirit) and baptism by fire.
- Tongues, prayer language, and gifts of the spirit
- The Church and the five-fold ministry
- Evangelism

- The Revelation of Jesus:
  - the rapture
  - the Judgement Seat of Christ
  - the tribulation
  - the marriage supper of the Lamb
  - the imminent return of Christ to the earth
  - the Battle of Armageddon the Millennium
  - the lake of fire where Satan will join his conspirators and anyone else who chooses the second death (not born again to salvation).
  - the White throne Judgement
  - the new Jerusalem
  - the lovely fruit-bearing trees on each side of the river of life for the healing of the nations.

There's so much more to include as we see God's way of caring for mankind. It's a panoramic view of His love for us and how His redemptive plan was compassionately executed. Of course, as mentioned, the plan was far more elaborate than we could ever know.

As we labor and work as servants for the Kingdom, we should consider the significance of God's creative order whenever we engage in ministry work, prayer, or in caring for others. There's a prescribed way to be in relationship with God that does not involve legalism but does require us to have a sincere heart of intimacy with God, love for our sisters and brothers, and honor.

When we're healthy in these areas of reverence and order, we're more apt to take better care of ourselves, enabling us to be healthy in our bones. As we allow the Holy Spirit to help bring a sense of holy order, watch God begin to move. As we lift the things of God in love, we'll remember to carefully live out our liberties in holiness.

I'm reminded of King David in his first attempt to bring the Ark of the Covenant to Jerusalem. We learn in 2 Samuel 6:1-11, that King David gathered all the choice men of Israel to bring the ark of God to Jerusalem. They played music on all kinds of instruments before the Lord, but when the oxen stumbled, Uzzah mishandled the ark. The Lord was angry with Uzzah because of his error, and he died there by the ark of God.

The Bible tells us that King David became angry and fearful because God had responded to Uzzah's error in an angered response. So, David would not move the ark. He brought it to the house of Obed Edom. There it remained for three months, and the Lord blessed Obed and his household. David found out about the blessings in Obed's household and went back to retrieve the ark of God. In 1 Chronicles 15:1-29, we see that this time David was prepared with instructions on how to handle the ark.

- He first prepared a place for the ark.
- The Lord had chosen only the Levites to carry the ark and to minister before Him.
- He gathered all Israel.
- He assembled the children of Aaron and the Levites in order with the others.
- He instructed the heads of the Levites to sanctify themselves and their brethren so that they might bring up the ark to the place that had been prepared.
- The children of the Levites bore the ark of God on their shoulders by its poles, as Moses had commanded according to the Word of the Lord.
- The leaders of the Levites appointed musicians for the occasion.

"For because you did not do it the first time, the Lord our God broke out against us, because we did not consult him about the proper order" (1 Samuel 15:13). King David was successful the second time around.

We have many outstanding examples in the Old Testament of how to be in relationship with God. God has not changed. As mentioned earlier, we now have Sonship with him through the blood of Jesus. As sons and daughters of the Most High, Ancient of Days (as Daniel would say—Daniel 7:9), and of Abba Father, our posture has shifted from people of a temporary sacrificial system of old, to that of free men and women functioning under grace and mercy by the blood of Jesus. In our new dispensation, we see that Jesus has fulfilled the requirements of the letter of the law.

As we endeavor to receive all the tender mercies that He so kindly bestowed upon us, including rewards in the eternal life, and freedom as we walk in this present abundant life, we pray that God would help us to honor all that he has done for us. We pray that we honor and care for one another, and that we're able to walk in peace, love, and order as we consider our sisters and brothers who may be either weak in the faith or have not yet received Jesus.

I will instruct you and teach you in the way you should go; I will guide you with my eye. do not be like the horse or the mule, which have no understanding, which must be harnessed with bit and bridle, else they will not come near you.

Psalm 32:8,9

We are to be sensitive to the Holy Spirit as He comforts and helps in times of distress. God is concerned about each one of us, and our households. He hasn't forgotten any one of us. Just as He planned out things from the beginning, He has a plan for every life.

Scripture reminds us how God remembered Noah after the flood. Noah may have thought he was forgotten in the ark, but God's Word contains promises for us, and He follows through on His Word (Genesis 8:1).

He remembered Rachel when she was barren and later blessed her with two children, Joseph and Benjamin (Genesis 3:22).

God remembered Abraham during the time of Sodom and Gomorrah when he thought his nephew Lot would be destroyed along with the city of Sodom. God rescued Lot and his daughters (Genesis 19:29).

Then there's Hanna who like Rachel was childless and desperately wanted a child. She was teased and taunted by her husband's other wife who had many children. Hanna was in "bitterness of soul." The Bible says that God had blocked her womb.

Sometimes the Lord will block our initiatives when they are not aligned with His plans. That doesn't always mean the answer is "No." It could mean it's not time yet as in the case of Hanna. Hanna had to get to a place, spiritually, where she would allow God to use her child to do His work. Once she prayed and found peace to do this, we're told that God remembered Hanna and she was then able to conceive. Her son, Samuel, became a judge and a prophet. The Lord visited Hanna again and she bore five other children (1 Samuel 1:19,20).

God's Word encourages us to keep hope alive; to keep trusting in Him despite the circumstances. Remember, there is nothing too hard for God and that would include whatever sickness or adversity you may be experiencing (Genesis 18:14; Jeremiah 32:17; Jeremiah 32:27).

Chapter 7

Rest

Healing and rest go hand in hand. Jesus gives us the rest we need when we cast our cares upon Him. When we give our worries to the Lord, and trust in Him as our source, we are in a better position to receive His promises. We hear about resting in His promises or entering His rest. Let's see what Scripture says about this.

When God created the world, He rested from His work on the seventh day. However, God's rest was an all-inclusive representation of many events yet to come.

- It was a portrayal of life under the Mosaic laws where Israel was instructed to remember the Sabbath and keep it holy; to rest from work on the seventh day. (Exodus 20:8-11, Exodus 34:21, Deuteronomy 5:12-15)
- Even though we're not under the Mosaic laws, we still need to set aside a day to rest and honor God and we still need to honor His moral codes. As mentioned earlier, they are expressive of God's character. When we take time to rest, it rejuvenates and refreshes us to be available to serve and pray in good health and strength. It allows us to enjoy quality time of recreation and fellowship with friends and family. God designed our bodies to do all that we need to do, then to observe a day of rest.

- We also find spiritual rest where, today, we understand that we rest from the works of the law. We now find grace in Jesus. Our salvation does not hinge upon our own righteousness, (we could never be righteous enough), but the righteousness of God. "For by grace you have been saved, through faith, and that not of yourselves; it is a gift of God, not of works, lest anyone should boast" (Ephesians 2:8,9). We no longer need to toil and spin and keep under the works of the law. We find rest in what Jesus did for us at the cross.

- We rest in His promises. In every promise of healing and deliverance, we can be certain that the promises are ours when we believe. In all the encouraging words of Scripture, we can find peace and be comforted. We can declare words of healing, provision, and protection over our lives and be confident in their treasured truths. His Words allow us to find the peace we need in order to rest in faith.

- In Matthew 11:28 Jesus says, "Come to me all you who labor and are heavy laden, and I will give you rest. Take my yoke upon you and learn from Me, for I am gentle and lowly in heart, and you will find rest for your souls. For My yoke is easy and my burden is light."

As mentioned, we can find true rest in Jesus. When we believe in Jesus and walk in obedience to His Word, we enter His rest. Hebrews 4:9,10 tells us that there yet remains a rest for the people of God. When we cease from the works of the law and simply believe Jesus is the Son of God who died for our sins, we can enter the rest that Jesus has graciously given us and find comfort and joy in His promises. When we lean into Jesus and trust Him to lead, we find all the rest we need.

Even when sickness, or any other adverse thing comes our way, we learn to take His yoke as we cast our cares upon Him. What does it mean to take His yoke upon us?

In Biblical times, a frame of wood called a yoke, was placed on oxen enabling the animals to balance the heavy load they carried. Likewise, Jesus is saying, "You don't have to carry your burdens. Take my yoke, latch on to me, and let me do the carrying. You rest and let me do the work. Just lean into Me and coast. Cast your cares upon Me, trust Me to carry the load. I will give you rest.

How do we lean into Jesus? We believe and obey God's Word. We confess Jesus as Lord and Savior. We walk by faith as we rest in Jesus.

I've learned not to worry or stress, but to find peace in the truth of God's Word. It's a tremendous weight lifted, knowing I can depend on Jesus to carry the load. It's not an easy task though. I always feel as though I must work and help carry.

Knowing how to rest speaks volume. It's a bold declaration of faith that says, "I believe God's Words and I'm acting on that belief! I surrender and will learn to depend on Jesus." Even if my healing has not manifested, the Word of God says that Jesus bore my sickness on the cross. Again, be sensitive to the Holy Spirit. Listen to hear how to rest and partake of your blessings.

This is not to say you become passive, complacent, or foolish. Remember faith comes by hearing the Word. Build your faith! Meditate on His Word! Know the promises. Get revelation knowledge of what God is saying. Be led by His Holy Spirit to gain wisdom, courage, and strength to sustain you as you trust God for your miracle. As mentioned earlier, the thing you have petitioned God for might come over time.

Rest in Jesus as you gain insight into what God is wanting to do in your life. He will care for you!

In John 11, we read about Lazarus who got sick and died. His sisters, Mary and Martha, sent for Jesus at the first sign of his ailment. Jesus was at Bethabara beyond the Jordon at the time. He waited two days then headed to Judea before going on to Bethany where Lazarus and his sisters lived—a total of four days.

Jesus told His disciples that He was glad that He was not there because this would be an opportunity for them to believe. Jesus gave us a glimpse that there may be times when healing, or a prayer request, might be delayed. Perhaps more time is needed for us to properly believe, receive, and grow.

We understand that Mary and Martha needed to wait with patience and rest in His teachings, which can be taxing when death looms. Yet we are encouraged by this example to wait on the Lord, even in extreme circumstances. The Holy Spirit will give wisdom to see how to navigate difficult situations.

By the time Jesus arrived, Lazarus was dead, and the crowd was mourning. Jesus wept for His friend. He wept at the mourners' impatience and unbelief. He wept that they lost focus and had forgotten all He had taught them; that during times of adversity, cling to His Holy Word and rest in Him with full assurance that He is there to help. (A message for all of us.)

He waited four days, but ultimately, Lazarus was raised from the dead. It may not be when or how we think it should be; nevertheless, God chooses to lead us to grow, bear fruit, and teach others His Kingdom principles. God knows things that we'll never know, so who are we that we should worry? Are we like unbelievers who worry and fret about the things of life? Jesus at Bethany with Lazarus, his sisters, and their friends, reminds us that we'll all die at some point and will be raised to either everlasting life or everlasting torment. We choose.

This event with Lazarus also prefigures Jesus' death and resurrection. John 11:45-57 tells us that after word got out about Lazarus being raised from the dead, the High Priest and the Jewish council were afraid the Romans would come and take away both their place and nation. John 11:53 says, "From that day on, they plotted to put Him to death."

This miracle of Lazarus was monumental because it stirred the hearts of the people to believe in the power of God, so much that it propelled the Jewish leaders to move forward with their plans to kill Jesus. Today, it's important for us to exhibit that same level of belief. To have that same stirring, where others will come to believe and we too might witness an outbreak of new believers. Not an uprising of the murder of an innocent man—though that was necessary—but a shakeup that delivers boldness to the church, coupled with an over-flowing, refilling of the Holy Ghost leading to great evangelism!

To have a supernatural occurrence is a powerful witness, as in the case of Lazarus. The Word tells of many miracles. As we begin to experience and see miracles in our personal lives and those around us, let us continue to grow our faith as we respond to the demonstrations and truths that we read in the Scripture.

It doesn't matter how grim the circumstance, rest assured that His Word is true, and He invites you to surrender that He might help you carry the load. Whatever the concern, the answer is on the way. As you continue to rest in Jesus, remember you've been indwelled by the power of the Holy Spirit. The power to depend on Jesus. The power to trust. The power to command sickness and infirmities to leave your body.

Carry the joy of Jesus as you rest, yet actively deploy your authority.

Chapter 8

Obedience, Faith and Believing

I love how God sees and knows our hearts. When Israel was searching for a king, God told Samuel in 1 Samuel 16:7, "The Lord does not see as man sees: for man looks at the outward appearance but the Lord looks at the heart." Though David did not fit the bill physically compared to his brothers, God chose him as king based on his heart.

Many years before King David, God called another man who had a heart of obedience, and faith to fulfill God's plan. God took notice of him and gave him instructions on how to carry out that plan. Abraham would then become the Father of Faith because he believed what God promised. God promised Abraham that he would have many descendants, even though at that time Abraham and Sarah were both old and they were childless. God knew Abraham's heart and He knows your heart too.

Abraham was ready, willing, and able to leave his present home and move to the place God had directed him to go. He asked no questions, He just moved. How awesome for us to be able to release fear and trust God in that way. Abraham knew that God would always provide a way for him and his family. Even when he detoured to Egypt in route to Canaan and found himself in a precarious situation, God rescued him.

He was abundantly blessed even though he did not consult God before the detour (Genesis 12:10-20; 13:1,2). This is not the prescribed way and I'm certain, subsequently, Abraham gained much wisdom concerning his misstep. Or was it a misstep?

There are things we won't always understand about the Providence of God. Abraham did not always know the details of the plan, but he had faith that God would provide aid in every encounter. He had times of impatience as with Hagar and Ishmael (Genesis 16), because he did not always understand the dynamics of God's spoken Word over his life; however, his character was of a man with unprecedented faith (Hebrews 11:8,9). Abraham's relationship and response to God reveals what an intimate relationship with God looks like.

Hebrews 11:1 gives us the biblical definition of faith: "The assurance of things hoped for, the conviction of things not seen." We are to maintain conviction that God's Word is true while exhibiting full assurance of what we're hoping for will come to pass even though we can't see it. Scripture tells us that it is impossible to please God without faith (Hebrews 11:6).

Abraham's story is an excellent depiction of what it means to have faith and to believe that God's Word is true. Abraham heard the call, was given very little instruction, and yet was obedient.

Abraham did not know the specifics of where he was going nor what the plan was, but he was willing, obedient, and faithful to heed the call. Even though he didn't know the end of the thing, he was aware that he had to take a step into the unknown in order to get the thing started. The same is true when we obey God. There might be a required action on our part for us to receive our answer. We might have to demonstrate our trust in God. Though God knows our heart, there are times when He will present an opportunity to learn something about ourselves as we walk out in faith. Perhaps something that we never fully recognized—a characteristic that might be a hindrance to spiritual growth or healing.

In Exodus, the children of Israel were given instructions on how to gather the manna (bread from heaven).

> *Then the LORD said to Moses, "Behold, I will rain bread from heaven for you. and the people shall go out and gather a certain quota every day, that I may test them, whether they will walk in my law."*

Exodus 16:4

Additionally, the Lord instructed them not to gather manna on the Sabbath, but to gather a double portion on the sixth day so as not to be out gathering on the Sabbath. Disobedience would hinder their relationship with God. And it did. Although today, we're led by the spirit and not the works of the law, God will still give us instructions relating to certain personal events, or principles, to help with our spiritual development. To teach us how to walk by faith and obedience. Sometimes God's instruction might seem challenging, unnecessary, or even ridiculous. But we can be confident that God's purpose is to settle us and to help us find the path leading to spiritual growth.

Can you envision the temptation of gathering more food than instructed in order to ensure adequate provision? The instruction was not just about setting aside a day to observe the Sabbath. It served to reveal their nature, to teach discipline, obedience, honor, and to trust Him for all their provisions. If we forget these things, God will use our day-to-day situations as challenges and instructions for us to grow and to learn to walk by faith.

At this juncture, the children of Israel had just witnessed the ten plagues of Egypt which God used so that Moses could bring Israel out of slavery and to demonstrate His power (Exodus chapters 7-9). They observed the parting of the Red Sea that they might pass through on dry land and escape Pharaoh's violent pursuit (Exodus 14).

Yet, they complained of not having food or water after celebrating this miraculous deliverance. In all this, God still rained down bread from heaven. He observed that they gathered more than instructed because they were fearful and did not trust His Word. Fear is a spirit that will rob intimacy with God. Hopefully these examples will help to demonstrate the importance of obedience, faith, and believing in Jesus for healing.

In 1 Kings 17, the widow of Zarephath had to step out in great faith in order to grant the prophet Elijah his request for a portion of her small meal during a time of drought and famine. Elijah, also, had to exhibit much boldness to request food when he was aware of the food shortage. He may have considered a possible backlash from the widow, even though God told Elijah, He had commanded her to share. In our natural thinking we might wonder, "Why would anyone give food to a stranger when there's only enough for one last meal for yourself and your child? And why would someone come to your house to ask, being fully aware of the famine?"

Elijah was hungry, so God told him to go to the woman and that He had commanded her to give him food. Elijah didn't remind God that there's a drought or that, "no one is sharing food these days." He was not timid, even though this was a Gentile woman who might blast him with words of insult. He did not walk in fear as he approached the woman. He went in faith, believing what God had told him.

When he arrived, the woman seemed somewhat hesitant, but was convicted to share because God had placed it in her heart. When the Providence of God allows change to produce a certain outcome, nothing can withstand Him. We do, however, have free will. But there are times when God will usurp our agency for matters relating to kingdom purposes.

We know that at that time Elijah was dealing with the unreasonable King Ahab, and his evil wife, Jezebel. They were in opposition to God's plans while killing God's priests. You can't fight God and expect to live a normal life. Prophecies were in place and had already been activated. When someone tries to thwart God's plans, revelation of His omnipotence is distinguishable, maybe more than any other times, because the motion has already been set.

The trajectory of God's plan is spiritually carved and can only be altered by God. That's not to say that God will force anyone to accept His invitation for salvation or obstruct the freedom of choice. However, when Kingdom plans are set, you either can align yourself with God's purposes or you can "kick against the goads" as the Apostle Paul did before he came to see the truth (Acts 9:5).

The widow woman had been commanded by God, to feed Elijah even though she had only a small amount of meal and oil. Elijah told her not to fear, but to make him a cake first, then to make some for herself and her son. (The faith that was necessary here is the same faith required for our healing today).

Why did the prophet tell her not to fear? As I said earlier, usually there was risk involved. The widow woman may have feared that the portion given to the prophet would eliminate the chance for her and her son to have their last meal. But she was willing to risk it even though she had no indication of how the food would be replaced.

The prophet encouraged her saying, "For thus says the lord God of Israel: the bin of flour shall not be used up, nor shall the jar of oil run dry, until the day the Lord sends rain upon the earth" (1 Kings 17:14). She believed him!

There is hope and encouragement in God's Word. Believe it! Let's look at the dynamics of this passage:

- Both had needs—Elijah needed food, the widow needed a food miracle and subsequently a healing for her son (1 Kings 17:17-24).
- They each heard from God
- Both had to be obedient
- Both had to walk by faith
- Both had to be encouraged—God encouraged Elijah, and Elijah encouraged the widow, saying, "Do not fear."
- Both had work to do—the widow to prepare food and prepare a room for him to stay. The prophet had to ultimately minister to the widow to save her son.
- The principle of *first* is mentioned in this passage. Put God first in all things, especially in giving. Matthew 6: 33 tells us to seek first the Kingdom of God and His righteousness and all these things shall be added to you. She did what was asked of her. She gave not knowing that she would be totally blessed.

- The widow woman gained a sense of obedience and faith. She believed and trusted God for provision. Ultimately, she witnessed the deliverance of her son from death. She grew in her knowledge of the God of Israel, who worked miracles on her behalf.
- For Elijah, as his ministry called for obedience, faith and faithfulness, commitment, good character and believing in God.

When we align ourselves with the plans and purposes of God, it becomes incumbent on us to participate and wholly rely on God in circumstances requiring great faith. When faced with adversity, or some challenging circumstance where God's instructions may not make sense, we are to declare His Word, hold onto our confession, and stand firm. Remember— the just shall live by faith (Romans 1:17). Whether it be for healing or any other concern in life.

Jesus gives us many examples of receiving healing by faith. The principle is clear: "When you believe, all things are possible" (Mark 9:23) This statement was made to the father of the boy whom the disciples had difficulty healing. Again, Jesus, upon ministering to the crowd at Lazarus' house, encouraged them with these words, "Did I not say to you that if you would believe, you would see the Glory of God?" (John 11:40)

One might ask, "What is the Glory of God?" Let's examine the context in which Jesus was speaking. He is quieting the crowd to encourage them to believe all that He has taught them. After He spoke to them about seeing the Glory of God, they took away the stone where Lazarus lay. Jesus prayed, allowing the people to hear his prayer, that they might believe He was sent by God. Then Lazarus came out of the grave! All who were there witnessed the supernatural power of God. From this perspective, it appears that the Glory of God has to do with the manifest presence and power of God. This event was so powerful that it triggered the plot to kill Jesus.

With all this, we are directed to obey and to walk by faith. Continue to believe His promises and declare your healing for He bore your sickness on the Cross. Be healed in the mighty name of Jesus!

Chapter 9

Walking in Faith

Remember the woman with the issue of blood. She did not sit around waiting for Jesus. When she heard about the miracles, she went looking for Him. She did not need anointing oil. She wasn't looking for hands to be laid on her. She purposed in her heart that if, "I could just touch his garment, I will be made whole" (Mark 5:28).

Though she seemed timid, she found faith in the face of sickness. This shows us that in the face of adversity we can find our way to God. Her faith raised her to a place which bolstered her boldness to go and receive her miracle—regardless of the societal codes. She went to meet Jesus! He had the power, and she had the faith.

This was a meeting twelve years in the making. Her isolated life of hurt and sorrow was revived by the Life-Giver. They crossed paths when He was in route to heal (bring life) to Jairus' daughter. The woman heard about the Messiah's power and compassion and was absolutely determined in her soul to be healed.

We are tremendously blessed to have this treasure of God's Word and His promises. Read the Word in order to know the promises! Faith comes by hearing the word.

You might be asking, "Where do I start? What do I need to do?" Start by believing that God's Word is true. Then build your faith by reading the Word and hearing the word. Take time to read. It's crucial. Begin to speak and declare God's Words and promises over your life, and over family members and friends. See the blessings and fruit of God's Word begin to transform areas of your life where you maybe had lost hope. Experience the vibrancy and beauty of God's Holy Word as it brings clarity, perspective, and a far deeper intimacy with God as you learn to walk by faith and not by sight.

Let's look at Mark 11:23,24. In this passage, Jesus is teaching the disciples how to pray and how, by faith, to speak to situations, while believing without doubting. In verse 23, the Word tells us that whoever says to the mountain, "Be removed," and does not doubt in his heart, but believes those things he says, he will have whatever he says.

The mountain may be a problem, or an illness. Jesus promises that whoever speaks to the mountain will have whatever he asks. Jesus is encouraging us to use our authority by faith. Jesus spoke to the fig tree by faith (Mark 11:12-14), and later He said to his disciples, "Whatever things you ask for when you pray, believe that you receive them, and you will have them" (Mark 11:24).

There's something else you'll need to do. Jesus says that when we pray, if we have anything against anyone, forgive so that our Father in heaven may also forgive our trespasses.

Faith is required to see prayers answered. It wouldn't be to any advantage to harbor unforgiveness. Unforgiveness can cancel or nullify our prayers. God is not honored when we carry bitterness. Unforgiveness and any act of defiance or disobedience hinders our walk of faith, causes us to be out of proper relationship with God, and hinders our ability to hear His voice. God deals with our heart.

Matthew 5:23,24 tells us, "If you bring your gift to the altar, and there remember that your brother has something against you, leave your gift there before the altar and go your way. First be reconciled to your brother, and then come and offer your gift."

As difficult as it is, Jesus tells us to resolve our disputes before presenting offerings before God. His desire is always for us to be peaceable and loving toward one another, so that we might be in a better relationship with Him. Prepare yourself before the Lord so that you can receive all His benefits. Don't let the foolishness of Satan's interferences and distractions keep you from receiving the blessings of Jesus. Remember, healing is His will for us. Matthew 9:29 tells us, "According to your faith let it be to you."

Matthew 8:5-13 talks about a Centurion who came to Jesus asking Him to heal his servant. He told Jesus that his servant was home, paralyzed, and dreadfully tormented. Jesus offered to come and heal him. The Centurion wouldn't hear of it.

He said, "Lord, I am not worthy that you should come under my roof. But only speak a word and my servant will be healed." The Centurion had an opportunity to have Jesus come to his house. But he was focused, determined, and filled with faith that if Jesus would just speak a word his servant would be healed.

In effect, he was saying, "Forget the visit, Lord, I'm not fit for you to come to my house. I am also a man under authority, having soldiers under me." He recognized that Jesus also had authority in the spiritual realm.

The Centurion was a Roman leader asking a Jewish Rabbi to heal his servant. The Centurion obviously believed what He had heard about Jesus. He was a man in desperate need of a word from the Messiah.

Jesus marveled at his faith and said to those who followed, "Assuredly, I say to you, I have not found such great faith, not even in Israel." Then Jesus said to the Centurion, "Go your way; and as you have believed, so let it be done for you." His servant was healed that same hour.

How awesome it must feel to have that kind of faith. Faith like the woman with the issue of blood that says, "Just let me touch his clothes," or faith like the centurion who says, "Just say a word, Jesus."

God allows these common, ordinary, faith-filled people to present us with examples of hope and encouragement. Examples where we learn to walk by faith while making significant strides, not only toward healing, but toward a more intimate relationship with Jesus. And as we walk, we remember the ten lepers including a Samaritan who came back to Jesus to say, "Thank you" (Luke 17:15-19).

Pray this prayer:

Thank you, Lord! We thank you for your healing power. Like the Samaritan, we thank you. Your Word tell us that we were healed by your stripes. We believe it, receive it, and we walk by faith to see the manifestation of our healing. We know it is your will for believers to live in whole health. We worship you Father for you are holy. We thank you and we praise you.

In Jesus' name, Amen.

Chapter 10

The Fear of The Lord—
Reverence, Honor and Obedience

*There was a man in the land of Uz, whose name was
Job; and that man was blameless and upright, and one
who feared God and shunned evil.*

Job 1:1

Scripture tells us in Isaiah 33:6 that the fear of the
Lord is His treasure. It pleases the Lord when we
live in obedience to His Word. The Lord places
great value on our commitment and honor because it keeps us
near to Him. Reverence and the holy fear of God is a
discipline that the Holy Spirit can help us carry out.

God treasures our holy fear because it cautions us to stay
vigilant so as not to fall prey to Satan's tactics. His mercy is
on those who fear Him. God has great compassion for us and
does not want us to give the enemies of God an occasion to
blaspheme Him, whereby we would suffer consequences as a
result of sin (2 Samuel 12:14). This holy fear is not the same
as the spirit of fear (filled with fright or terror). The spirit of
fear is a clear impediment to your healing and will hinder
your faith.

Patricia Simon

The fear of the Lord is a decision to obey, honor, and reverence the holiness of God. The Holy Spirit gives us the strength we need to conduct ourselves accordingly as we respond to His Word. This strength that comes from the power of the Holy Ghost, also serves as a restraint mechanism helping to guard against our sin nature when we walk in the spirit, thus keeping us from the traps of Satan.

Who is the man that fears the Lord? Him shall He teach in the way He chooses. He himself shall dwell in prosperity, and his descendants shall inherit the earth. The secret of the Lord is with those who fear Him, And He will show them His covenant.

Psalm 25:12-14

What then, is the secret of the Lord? One thing's for sure, the fear of the Lord brings intimacy with God. Within the circle of intimacy, you come to understand how to seek the face of God, how to enter His gates with thanksgiving and how to love and have compassion for others even when they have wronged you.

- The fear of the Lord is the beginning of knowledge (Proverbs 1:7)
- The fear of the Lord is to hate evil (Proverbs 8:13)
- The fear of the Lord is the beginning of wisdom (Proverbs 9:10)
- The fear of the Lord is a fountain of life (Proverbs 14:27)
- Better is little with the fear of the Lord, than great treasure with trouble (Proverbs 15:16)

In Job's discourse on wisdom in Job 28:28, it reads: "Behold, the fear of the Lord, that is wisdom and to depart from evil is understanding."

Job had the wisdom to know that the holy fear of God keeps us walking in righteous living and turning away from sin. Today, because of the finished work of Jesus on the Cross, the Holy Spirit enables us to shun evil and to fear the Lord. When we walk in that truth, we gain the wisdom and discernment needed to make right choices, and making right choices is essential for good health and proper spiritual growth. Job didn't have a mediator, or the blood of Jesus. He chose to fear the Lord based on all that he heard about God. The Lord took notice of him, but so did Satan.

One might ask, if Job had the fear of the Lord but still got sick and had multitudes of trouble, how does it benefit a person to have the fear of the Lord? God knows us better than we know ourselves. Because of Job's righteousness and commitment to God, integrity was ingrained in his spirit despite the circumstances. God was well aware that Job was steadfast and would endure this monumental journey.

No temptation has overtaken you except such as is common to man: but God is faithful, who will not allow you to be tempted beyond what you are able, but with the temptation will also make the way of escape, that you may be able to bear it.

1 Corinthian 10:13

We will still have difficulties. We've come to know that suffering and trials are a fact of life. How we respond, and what is in our heart, can oftentimes have a great impact on the measure of our suffering. Again, the question may be, "If the most righteous man on earth at that time was bombarded with intense suffering, what chance do we have?"

Remember, Job's suffering was not a result of unrighteous conduct but as that of a man who had the holy fear of God. With this in mind, we must know that God had a purpose and plan for Job. We witness the attack of Satan as we read the book. The devil is the prince of the air, but God is in charge and has final say of all things.

> *Beloved, do not be surprised at the fiery trial that has come upon you, as though something strange were happening to you. But rejoice that you share in the sufferings of Christ, so that you may be overjoyed at the revelation of His glory.*
>
> 1 Peter 4:12, 13

Here's the thing, we know that from adversity, spiritual growth is inevitable. Even though Job did nothing wrong, the devil was not going to let up. Satan's interference did not diminish Job's commitment to God either. After the destruction of Job's property and the killing of his children, he worshipped God and said, "Naked I came from my mother's womb, and naked I shall return. The Lord gave and the Lord has taken away: blessed be the name of the Lord" (Job 1:21). When Satan came at Job the second time to attack his health, the Lord reminded Satan of how Job is one who fears God and shuns evil (Job 2:3).

How magnificent it is to have God speak of us in the same manner. To say He can depend on us to be loyal to the cause no matter what, even to the point of death. When we purpose

God's Kingdom plans in our heart, it reveals the depth of our commitment while strengthening and emboldening our faith. We are told throughout the Bible to fear the Lord. Here's what we can learn from this.

- We're better able to resist Satan and his devices when we fear the Lord.
- We find humility to walk in obedience.
- We find comfort and peace as God's Word is revealed in our lives.
- We develop greater faith.
- We find deeper intimacy with God.
- We're more inclined to declare His Word and promises for ourselves and others.
- We depend on Him for our healing and any other petitions we might have.
- We seek His face (His righteousness, His glory, His presence, and His will for our lives).
- We seek to please Him and honor Him not only for bestowing on us the greatest gift of love we have ever known, but we honor Him for who He is. His love for us also provided healing at the Cross. Our love for Him should reflect gratitude and honor.
- It's important to honor God by taking care of our bodies, our temple. We seek His face in response to His faithfulness to love and forgive us. The Holy Spirit reveals the holiness of our Father that we might respond with a bold desire to serve, honor, and fear the Lord.

Psalm 130:3,4 tells us, "If you, Lord, should mark iniquities, O Lord, who could stand? But there is forgiveness with You, that You might be feared."

Let's pray that fear translates to honoring God. Honor that causes us to exercise restraint in all that we do. When we exercise restraint, we take time to make better choices, including decisions about our bodies. We've been anointed to be able to discern and to practice wisdom when dealing with the issues of life.

Let's be wise to implement a healthy food program that includes conscious and deliberate choices, portion control, along with prayer and fasting. We should also have a sense, an awareness, and an acknowledgement that "Your body is the temple of the Holy Spirit" (1 Corinthians 6:19).

When we take care to treat our bodies properly, we are honoring God for sending Jesus to die not only for our sins, but also for bearing our sickness and hurt. As we honor God by caring for our body, we remember to forgive others. Unforgiveness hinders prayers, causes sickness and can diminish every aspect of the Christian walk. Worry and anxiety also contribute to lingering illnesses and reveal a lack of trust in God.

Job got a little testy toward the end of his suffering. Though after his second attack from Satan where he was afflicted with boils, Job stayed steadfast once again. His wife advised him to curse God and die, but he said to her, "You speak as one of the foolish women speaks. Shall we indeed accept good from God, and shall we not accept adversity?" In all this Job did not sin with his lips (Job 2:10).

It wasn't until the third attack which Satan brought on him, that made Job question his birth. When friends look at you and their accusatory eyes begin to question your righteousness, that's a sad event.

Before his troubles, the community held Job in high regard. Though Job suffered from his losses, and pain from the boils, his real agony came from the reaction of people. We know Job never did anything wrong to bring on this trial. It was Satan and his desire for power and destruction and an attempt to influence the believer's integrity and their faith to God.

Sickness and loss come in many different forms and for many different reasons. Take time to talk to God about your personal experiences. Let the Holy Spirit minister to you so that you might gain insight concerning your healing. Start with right believing of God's Holy Word. He wants you healed. Forgive, forgive, forgive! "Vengeance is mine says the Lord" (Romans 12:19). Search your thoughts and actions to see if you have areas of disobedience. Don't let ill feelings and anger rob you of your healing, peace, and joy. God is true to His Word. Let's stay true to Him!

Pray this prayer:

> You bore my sickness on the Cross, Lord, and by your stripes we were healed! If you are for me, who can be against me? No weapon formed against me shall prosper. Your words are health to all my flesh. Thank you, Father, for my complete, total healing.
>
> In Jesus' name, Amen.
>
> (1 Peter 2:24; Romans 8:31; Isaiah 54:17; Proverbs 4:20-23)

Job forgave his accusers and recognized that even though he was a man who feared the Lord and despised evil, there's always room for improvement. Job's trial was not due to error on his part, but his trial did expose faulty areas. He declared that due to his righteous living, he should be exempt from suffering. "Make me know my transgression and my sin. Why do you hide your face and regard me as your enemy?" (Job 13:24)

One truth that did surface was when Job proclaimed that he did not know how to contend with Almighty God. He indicated his need for a mediator, which revealed our absolute necessity for our Savior, Jesus. Subsequently, Job beheld a new revelation of God and recognized his error of trying to lean to his own understanding of who God is. Ultimately, Job repented. He began to see God through a different lens. As a result of his suffering, Job had a fresh revelation of God.

Today, Jesus helps us to see the Father, with Jesus himself being revealed in the Word. Jesus taught us how to see Him in Scripture as we witness in the passage that is often referred to as *The Road to Emmaus* (Luke 24:13-35). Verse 27 says, "And beginning at Moses and all the Prophets, He expounded to them in all the Scriptures the things concerning Himself."

We learn from Jesus that we should carry reverential fear of God, and allow the power of the Holy Spirit to open our eyes, open our understanding, and open the Word. When this happens, we come to a place where, like Job, the glory and revelation of who God is, enables us to find peace and faith to receive all that has already been poured out. This includes healings of every kind because all kinds were exchanged at the Cross—physical, mental, emotional, relational, and all other needs. We can open our hearts and allow God to speak as He did to Job. Then we witness the magnificent results of that spiritual transaction as we behold His righteousness and the abundant life that He sets before us.

The Bible tells us to resist the devil; it also tells us to fear the Lord. When we walk in obedience and reverence toward the Lord, we establish better intimacy with the Father. This encourages us to enter His presence with boldness, not only to ask our petitions, but also to seek His face, causing us to live with integrity and honor just as Job did. Also, allowing us to be wholly healed and fully restored.

Chapter 11

Humility

As believers, the way we live should resemble the life of Jesus. The encounters Jesus had with the people of that day radiated humility. From His teaching on taking the lowly place in Luke 14:7-14, to the surrendered garden cry, in Mark 14:36: "Abba father, all things are possible for You. Take this cup from Me; nevertheless, not what I will, but what You will."

From the washing of the disciple's feet (John 13), to the triumphal entry on a donkey into Jerusalem, "Jesus made himself of no reputation, taking the form of a bond servant and coming in the likeness of men" (Philippians 2:7). Always know, that however God chooses to move in our lives, all glory goes to Him.

It's important to humble ourselves before God as we walk in the spirit. This walk will include showing humility to our fellowman, even with our enemies, because we can turn souls to Jesus when we are tender-loving and humble.

Let love be without hypocrisy. Abhor what is evil. Cling to what is good. Be kindly affectionate to one another with brotherly love, in honor giving preference to one another; not lagging in diligence, fervent in spirit, serving the Lord;

rejoicing in hope, patient in tribulation, continuing steadfastly in prayer; distributing to the needs of the saints, given to hospitality.

Bless those who persecute you; bless and do not curse. Rejoice with those who rejoice, and weep with those who weep. Be of the same mind toward one another. Do not set your mind on high things but associate with the humble. Do not be wise in your own opinion.

Repay no one evil for evil. Have regard for good things in the sight of all men. If it is possible, as much as depends on you, live peaceably with all men. Beloved, do not avenge yourselves, but rather give place to wrath; for it is written, "Vengeance is Mine, I will repay," says the Lord. Therefore "If your enemy is hungry, feed him; If he is thirsty, give him a drink; For in so doing you will heap coals of fire on his head." Do not be overcome by evil but overcome evil with good.

Romans 12:9-21

The Bible tells us to "humble yourself" as if to say, you have instructions and you have everything you need to confess Jesus as your Lord and Savior. You have the promises of God, you have the Holy Spirit, and you are well equipped to know how to conduct yourselves accordingly. If you do otherwise, straying from what you know, then you open the door to adversity and the possibility of having to "be humbled." So, it's highly recommended that you "humble yourself." (James 4:10 and 1 Peter 5:6)

In simple terms, live a life lined up with the passage above in Romans. Rehearse it, internalize it and act on it! Begin to value God's Word over other influences. Humility does not compromise truth and will not allow us to esteem ourselves over others. In Matthew 18:1-5, Jesus was asked, "Who is the greatest in the kingdom of heaven?" Jesus calls a child to him and says, "Whoever humbles himself as this little child is the greatest in the kingdom of heaven."

I'm reminded of Jonah who fled from his calling. We don't know a whole lot about Jonah other than he did not want to go to evangelize the people of Nineveh—the most cruel and wicked nation of that day. Jonah knew that his people were the chosen people and seemingly he did not want others to experience this relationship with the God of creation.

We can't hold Jesus to ourselves; we must have compassion for souls. This means Kingdom work will call us from our comfort zones to minister to individuals or groups that are vulnerable, cruel, or different than we are.

It's hard to know if Jonah was filled with pride because pride takes on many different forms, but he certainly was not humble. He had to be humbled even at the cost of possible death. While Jonah lay in the belly of the great fish, he cried out to God as he recalled how God had delivered him from the raging sea, transitioning him from death to life. He prayed to the Lord:

"When my soul fainted within me, I remembered the Lord; and my prayer went up to You, into your holy temple. Those who regard worthless idols (when we turn from God to put out trust in false vanities) forsake their own mercy (a sure source of hope). But I will sacrifice to you with the voice of thanksgiving; I will pay what I have vowed. Salvation is of the Lord."

Jonah 2:7-9

> 123

So, the Lord spoke to the fish, and it vomited Jonah onto dry land. Jonah fulfilled his mission. However, he experienced post-evangelism trauma, because he simply did not understand the love God has for unbelievers. Pride and disobedience can lead us to have to be humbled as Jonah was and can bring unwarranted trouble to those around us—as it did with the people on the boat with Jonah. God cared for the people of Nineveh. He had great compassion for them. We are the laborers and workers—the hands and feet of Jesus—who must honor and glorify God by ministering to others, the compassion of Christ.

I never knew how to pray to have humility because it usually came through hardship of some kind, and I am not one to willingly sign up for pain. So then, exactly how do we acquire this attribute of all attributes? How is having humility conducive to our healing?

Remember, the Lord deals with our heart. Defilement comes from within our spirit person and is a hindrance to our healing. It places bondage upon you and causes you to be filled with pride. Pride falsely elevates and exalts to a place of idolatry where your inclination is to worship everything concerning self. You'll have no genuine interest in fostering hope or helping to develop others in their spiritual walk. You might be deceived into believing that your behavior is instrumental for the enrichment of those around you, but your actions reveal otherwise. This behavior will weigh on you.

It's difficult to hear the Father's voice when we're weighed down. Jonah had to be in the stillness of a fish before he was able to see his conduct clearly. When Satan comes at you with ideas of superiority, self-righteousness, or any false humility, steer clear (resist) and know that your righteousness is in Jesus.

James 4:6 tells us that, "God resists the proud but gives grace to the humble." God tells us that friendship with the world is enmity with him (James 4:4). The *world* meaning that Satan is the ruler of this world. Many people abide in unbelief and are disassociated with the things of God, causing them to engage in unrighteous behavior. God wants us to love and care for the unbeliever, but not to fall prey to Satan's deceptions thus becoming part of the foolishness.

When I first read the words, "humble yourself" in Scripture, I felt somewhat anxious as if there were something else, I needed to do in addition to abiding in His Word. I wasn't sure how to navigate prayer in the arena of humility. I decided to simply pray that Holy Spirit would help me to "know humility." Yet, being aware that even the concept of praying to "know humility" still conjured up thoughts of some kind of vicious trial. I continued to pray that way because I understood the necessity of having humility since it contrasts with pride.

I came to see that humility is not that elusive thing (you strive for it, but you don't know when or if you have it), that I thought it was. I didn't have to tremble at the idea of humbling myself. When we apply God's Word of wisdom to our lives, humility and other attributes become a natural part of our spiritual growth. Inevitably, even though we might be committed Christians, there'll be times we still need to be humbled in order to see when we're in error and correct a particular behavior, thus clearing the way for more growth.

What does humility have to do with sickness? Everything. Earlier, I talked about Adam and Eve, and how sickness was a result of their disobedience. Our sin nature invites sickness. God hates pride and foolishness, and we need God's Holy Spirit to help us navigate God's righteous way. Live His Word and declare His promises over your life and your body. When we stray from that, we become complacent and lukewarm to the point where God has to look for us the way he did Adam and Jonah. Of course, He knew where they were, but they were spiritually separated. It's important to stay watchful, bold, and humble while remembering the authority we have in Jesus' name. When we're in right relationship with God, we earnestly seek His presence, power, and protection and all other benefits. When not, we veer off and become distracted.

I still tremble at the thought of having to be humbled, but it comes with the territory. Trials truly are inevitable and most often necessary. God is a Holy God and deals with us in holiness because Jesus made us righteous. When we act otherwise, steps are taken to help us remember who we are in Christ. It's a beautiful undertaking when sometimes we must be chastised and humbled as a result of our un-Christ-like behavior.

Hebrews 12:5,6 tells us, "My son, do not despise the chastening of the Lord, nor be discouraged when you are rebuked by Him. For whom the Lord loves he chastens." Again, God wants us whole and filled with the joy of Jesus. He does not want us to hurt or suffer. Unlike Job, our suffering tends to come from our own carelessness and disobedience. We can avoid many of our illnesses when we trust God, stay faithful to His Word, and remain humble, in the same spirit of humility that Jesus embraced in the Garden and on the Cross.

Chapter 12

Self Restraint

G od's redemptive plan of Genesis 3:15, gave the world hope. As the declaration went forth, it was carried by the spirit so that it paved the way for God's people to get into expectation to receive the King. It stirred the hearts and minds of the Patriarchs to give attention to the Word, to teach their children to stay vigilant and focus on the cause. When King David went to fight Goliath, he said to his brother who was trying to discourage him, "Is there not a cause?" (1 Samuel 17:29)

David was only a teenager at the time. God's timing—by way of his father Jesse—brought David to the scene of the battle to bring sustenance for his brothers. When David heard this pagan giant speaking blasphemous words against the armies of God, he was filled with holy indignation. David had many causes and convictions that day as he was sent out to the battlefield—to silence the enemies of Israel, to bring honor to the living God, and to keep hope alive for the Genesis 3:15 declaration.

Whether or not David understood the impact of this defeat, is irrelevant. He understood there was a greater cause other than obeying his father. No matter the battle, It's the cause that propels us to step out and do exploits like David did. We may not always understand, and surely we will have those who criticize. But for us today, we know that Jesus died for our sins and will return to receive us to eternal life. So, we need to be prepared, to show care and concern for others and to remember the cause: The Imminent Return of Christ.

On the journey of old, when many lost the passion for the cause, the remnant hung in there. They were confident that on down the road there was coming a King, a Savior, a Redeemer Who would save Israel from her persecutors and captors, with the larger portrait being the mystery of Christ which was salvation for Jews and Gentiles.

Jesus would defeat the enemy and deliver all His people from sin. The first defeat would take place as our Redeemer would come to the world to set the people free from indwelling sin and restore sonship. Jesus won the victory for our salvation. This proclamation put Satan on notice that his tactics and deceptions would no longer be tolerated because the people are now equipped with authority in the name of Jesus to help in everyday living. The second defeat will occur at the end of days when Satan will be bound for a thousand years in the bottomless pit prior to his eternal destruction in the lake of fire (Revelation 20:1-4; 7-10).

Jesus, as our Redeemer, came to us bearing humility, but He also came with another awesome trait. He exhibited a strength, a robust self-restraint that afforded Him the spiritual dynamics needed to finish the work. Like His other attributes, this self-restraint was meant for us to imitate. How? What kind of power is needed for us to behave like Jesus?

As has been said previously, He has equipped us with everything we need to live an abundant life: forgiveness of sins, wholeness, protection, provision, and the wisdom to know to humble ourselves. Remember though, He gave us a special gift to help us as we journey. The Holy Spirit helps to facilitate every situation we might encounter. If God tells us to resist the devil, then we can resist the devil with the power of the Holy Spirit. So then, we can exercise restraint in everyday circumstances. The actual process of finding restraint is akin to finding humility, living accordingly is always the answer. Our Lord and Savior could have thrown in the towel on many occasions but understood the mission and what was hanging in the balance:

- Starting with Jesus' temptation by Satan, Mark tells us that Jesus was in the wilderness forty days with the wild beasts; and the angels ministered to Him. He hadn't eaten. He could have called it quits at this juncture. He fought Satan with truth and kept going.
- He was rejected by his family and friends at Nazareth.
- His cousin, John the Baptist, was beheaded and yet, Jesus continued His work.
- He withstood continuous persecution.
- In Mark 8:31, Jesus began to teach his disciples that the Son of Man must suffer many things and be rejected by the elders and chief priests and scribes and be killed and after three days rise again. Peter began to rebuke Him. Jesus said to Peter, get behind me, Satan! For you are not mindful of the things of God, but the things of men. How difficult it must have been to tell your followers of your impending death following all the miracles and still no clear answers of liberation from the Roman influence.
- He meets the Samaritan woman at the well. He hadn't eaten. The disciples were trying to get Him to eat. He replied, "My food is to do the will of

Him who sent Me, and to finish his work." (John 4:34)

- The Triumphal Entry, (Palm Sunday) where Jesus went to Jerusalem on a donkey the week before His crucifixion knowing He would be arrested.
- The Garden of Gethsemane
- The crown of thorns
- Observing the faces of His mother and John as He continued to build relationship and community even while on the Cross. Yet, not losing sight of the cause or the mission.
- Enduring the piercings and the horror.

We see here a self-restraint that is uncommon to man. However, it is attainable because the Bible tells us in Hebrews 4:15-16 that we have a High Priest who can sympathize with our weaknesses. In all points He was tempted as we are. Let us therefore come boldly to the throne of grace, that we may obtain mercy and find grace to help in time of need.

We find this challenging because we have many factors operating against us. We have the world and all its temptations—the lust of the flesh, the lust of the eyes, and the pride of life (1 John 2:16). How does one escape? We get geared up! We put on the armor described in Ephesians 6, and we discipline ourselves to the truths contained in God's Word. Then we set our minds on the awesomeness of what Christ has done for us, recognizing that there is something far more important than pacifying our desire to live this life our way. That there's a surrendering that must occur, a brokenness that will settle and establish us. Once we come to this maturity, we're able to witness a self-restraint in our spirit that is sweet, refreshing, restful, and yet, still sometimes very challenging.

God has placed inside of each one of us the ability to say "No." To resist. To resist the occasion to engage in sinful behavior that could open the door to chaos and sickness. To resist the opportunity to overeat or eat unhealthy foods which can cause various diseases. To use restraint when the enemy flashes a way to gain wealth by ungodly means which can cause stress and worry. To be able to look away when presented with countless temptations that wears heavy on our heart health and our relationship with God.

> *For God may speak in one way or in another, yet man does not perceive it. In a dream, in a vision of the night, when deep sleep falls upon men, while slumbering on their beds, then He opens the ears of men, and seals their instruction. In order to turn man from his deeds. And conceal pride from man. He keeps back his soul from the Pit.*
>
> Job 33:14-18

God also places inside of us the ability to carry out His Kingdom plans in good health. No matter the weapons formed against us and despite the trials, He planted a spirit of victory because the battle is already won. Our work is to believe and walk by faith thereby allowing the Holy Spirit to do His work as we walk in full assurance that Jesus is the Healer and has borne all our sufferings on the Cross. We can be healed in the Name of Jesus. We can lift our hands and begin to thank God and praise Him that He loved us to whole health bearing all our hurt. Love Him and love your neighbor. Let's humble ourselves and find the self-restraint we need to stay in obedience and in the will of God.

Part II

Hindrances and Barriers to Healing

In Part II of *Healing in His Wings: Honoring and Embracing God's Promises,* we will explore areas in our lives that could possibly create hindrances and barriers to the healing process. It's crucial that these be given an honest evaluation. We know the enemy's ploy is to be subtle. He tricked Eve by using God's Word, but with just a bit of falsity. He will attempt to trick us in the same way.

There can be ongoing prayer for healing, and if it is not manifested the assumption might be that "healing isn't for today." Or perhaps one might believe the lie that "God is trying to teach me something with this malady."

Rather than taking this route, let's courageously dig deeper and review this list of possible hindrances one at a time.

- Pride
- Doubt and Unbelief
- Unforgiveness
- The Spirit of Fear
- Stress and Worry
- Discouragement, Disappointment, or Bitterness

Patricia Simon

- Self-Reliance
- Disobedience and Sin
- Demonic Oppression
- Other Strongholds

Pride

Pride is tops among the things God hates (Proverbs 6:16-19) and could certainly be a barrier to healing. There is, obviously, a healthy pride where someone might have reasonable confidence in personal accomplishments such as excitement over achievements made by a family member, or the successful outcome of a particular task.

The pride that God hates is when we take our successes or achievements to another level; when the admiration of oneself becomes excessive to the point of self-worship and feelings of superiority, arrogance, or conceit. Whether or not pride is a feeling, spirit, or emotion, it has detrimental effects on our well-being.

In Acts 10, Peter is given a vision from God showing that Peter should call no man common or unclean. Peter then presented the gospel to Cornelius and other Gentiles in his household.

> *Then Peter opened his mouth and said: "In truth I perceive that God shows no partiality. But in every nation whoever fears Him and works righteousness is accepted by Him. The word which God sent to the children of Israel, preaching peace through Jesus Christ—He is Lord of all..."*
>
> Acts 10:34-36

Peter was justifiably proud of his heritage, and also his obedience to all of the Jewish dietary rules, and rules of never entering into the home of a Gentile. Now he had to lay down that pride and learn what God was saying.

Where does the spirit of self-admiration, and the lifting of oneself come from? When Jesus was in the wilderness for forty days, we get a glimpse of the nature of Satan (Mark 1:12,13). He wants to be idolized and worshipped. In order to achieve this, he devises schemes to deceive God's people. The Bible tells us that Satan was an angel in heaven before his earthly mischief.

Ezekiel pronounces judgements on the King of Tyre whose heart was lifted up, declaring himself as God. As we continue reading of the lamentations of the King of Tyre, we get a background of Satan's time as an angel in heaven. Though Satan still has access to heaven, he is not the anointed angel that he once was. God used the prophet Ezekiel to speak these lamentations for the King of Tyre, of whom it is believed was empowered by Satan.

You were the seal of perfection, full of wisdom and perfect in beauty. You were in Eden, the garden of God; every precious stone was your covering: the sardius, topaz, and diamond. beryl, onyx and jasper, sapphire, turquoise, and emerald with gold. The workmanship of your timbrels and pipes (reference to Satan's musical talents) was prepared for you on the day you were created. You were the anointed who covers, I established you; you were on the holy mountain of God; you walked back and forth amid fiery stones. You were perfect in your ways from the day you were created, till iniquity was found in you.

Ezekiel 28:1-26

As mentioned, Satan's goal is to be worshipped. Let's see what the prophet Isaiah says: "How you are fallen from heaven, o lucifer, son of the morning! How are you cut down to the ground. You who weakened the nations!"

Here are the five *I wills* of Satan found in this passage (Isaiah 14:12-15):
1. I will ascend into heaven.
2. I will exalt my throne above the stars of God.
3. I will also sit on the mount of the congregation on the farthest side of the north.
4. I will ascend above the heights of the clouds.
5. I will be like the Most High.

We can see that the spirit of self-exultation comes from Satan. As stated, he uses deceptive traps to lure us into an attitude of superiority and conceit. We must be watchmen over our own conduct, because the devil schemes to cause animosity in relationships with family, friends, and especially our relationship with God.

Pride destroys. If you feel that you have broken relationships because you have difficulty saying, "I'm sorry," remember that the Spirit of God inside you is greater than the spirit of pride.

Humble yourself to apologize, then use your God-given authority to believe and command pride to leave. Believing can be the difficult part. Ask God to help you to not be vulnerable to the devil's foolishness, but to be vigilant according to His instructions in 1 Peter 5:8.

Part of commanding the spirit of pride to leave might involve your having to confront other deep-seated issues or strongholds. Jesus is the Healer. He will help you through whatever you're facing. If your situation is extreme, ask your pastor or leader to help you work through your issues.

As mentioned earlier, we are sometimes sick because of negative thoughts and behaviors we cling to, which most often come under the umbrella of pride. This is not to say we won't have legitimate hurts where we need more in-depth counseling. Ask God to guide you and direct you to the right people.

Is any among you afflicted? let him pray. Is any merry? let him sing psalms. Is any sick among you? let him call for the elders of the church; and let them pray over him, anointing him with oil in the name of the Lord: And the prayer of faith shall save the sick, and the Lord shall raise him up; and if he have committed sins, they shall be forgiven him.

James 5:14,15

The other part of that passage tells us to confess our trespasses to one another and pray for one another that you may be healed. The effectual, fervent prayer of a righteous man avails much (James 5:16). Here, we can stand strong in prayer with other believers to receive our healing.

However, as mentioned above, if your situation warrants a deeper intervention or anointing, seek the elders in your fellowship. In the same passage in James 5, we're given an example of how Elijah prayed for it to not rain, and it did not rain on the land for three years and six months. He prayed again and the earth gave rain. We can pray and call on God just like Elijah did and see magnificent results.

Pride causes hurt and division. Cast it down in the name of Jesus! Below are several Scriptures regarding pride.

The fear of the lord is to hate evil. Pride and arrogance and the evil way and the perverse mouth I hate.

Proverbs 8:13

When pride comes, then comes shame; but with the humble is wisdom.

Proverbs 11:2

Pride goes before destruction, and a haughty spirit before a fall.

Proverbs 16:18

Let each of you look out not only for his own interest, but also for the interest of others.

Philippians 2:4

God resists the proud but gives grace to the humble.

James 4:6

Pray this prayer:

Father, one way we've learned to cast down pride and to humble ourselves, is to live according to your Holy Word. We know to be filled with pride can be a challenging ordeal because we can't always see our arrogance or self-admiration. We need your help with this. We pray for vigilance to stay focused because we know the enemy wields a deceptive sword to either keep us in bondage or to destroy us.

We call out that spirit of pride to flee and never to return! We ask for total deliverance. Help us to not exalt ourselves above others, but to attend to the needs of our sisters and brothers with lovingkindness. Strengthen us to open our eyes to recognize our failings and make corrections so that our lives will be marked with love and will reflect the compassion of Jesus.

Help us to yield to your righteous ways as we continue to serve you with gladness. We pray that your Holy Spirit will help us in areas where humility is lacking and to be confident that we can do all things through Christ who strengthens us. Thank you for mercy, power, and love. Forgive our sins as we forgive one another.

In Jesus name, Amen.

Doubt and Unbelief

Herein lies the crux of many illnesses: doubt and unbelief. While the two are different, they can work hand-in-hand. First, we'll look at what the Word says about doubt.

Doubt

And Peter answered Him and said, Lord, if it is you, command me to come to you on the water." So, He said, "come," and when Peter had come down out of the boat, he walked on the water to go to Jesus. but when he saw that the wind was boisterous, he was afraid; and beginning to sink, he cried out, saying, "Lord save me!" and immediately, Jesus stretched out His hand and caught him, and said to him, "O you of little faith, why did you doubt?"

Matthew 14:28—31

So, the other disciples told Him, "We have seen the Lord!" Thomas replied, "unless I see the nail marks in His hands and put my finger where the nails were, and put my hands into His side, I will not believe.

John 20:25

But when you ask, you must believe and not doubt, because the one who doubts is like a wave of the sea, blown and tossed by the wind.

James 1:6

Next, we'll look at how the Word talks about unbelief.

Unbelief

Now he did no mighty work there because of their unbelief.

Matthew 13:58

Then the disciples privately said, "Why could we not cast it out?" Jesus said to them, "because of your unbelief; for assuredly, I say to you, if you have faith as a mustard seed, you will say to this mountain, 'move from here to there,' and it will move; and nothing will be impossible. However, this kind does not go out except by prayer and fasting.

Matthew 17:19,20

He who believes and is baptized will be saved; but he who does not believe will be condemned.

Mark 16:16

Beware, brethren, lest there be in any of you an evil heart of unbelief in departing from the living God.

Hebrews 3:12

Pray this prayer:

Father, doubt and unbelief keep us from experiencing Your goodness. It robs us of the peace and joy that comes with knowing You as Abba Father. It curses our lives and family because we haven't taken the time out of our existence to know you. Not only having knowledge of you but knowing you as a result of spending time in your Word.

There are times when we are overwhelmed with doubt, and we have difficulty believing because the depth of our trials may extend beyond our ability to accept the truth of your Word. When trouble takes our focus or we're sitting in the hospital room with a sick friend or relative, our faith gets shaky. During these times, may we be encouraged by the words you spoke to Thomas, "Because you have seen me, you have believed: blessed are those who have not seen and yet have believed" (John 20:29).

We repent for having a spirit of unbelief. You have given us many words and promises on believing, but we are sometimes slow to respond. Help us to believe and to have child-like faith that we may indulge in the impossible made possible. We cast down the spirit of doubt and unbelief. We walk by faith and not by sight. We expect the moving of your almighty hand among your people, where we witness and experience the supernatural power of God which includes healing of every kind of sickness under the sun.

In Jesus' name, Amen

Unforgiveness

G od deals with the heart. It's difficult to fully grasp the depth to which unforgiveness can defile a person. Bitterness in the heart will affect prayers and faith and will keep a person in continual distress. Forgiveness is not difficult, but the enemy would make us think so. Nothing is so freeing as cutting out a root of bitterness that has taken hold of the heart. Use these scriptures as an anchor while walking the journey of forgiveness.

Pursue peace with all people, and holiness, without which no one will see the Lord: looking carefully lest anyone fall short of the grace of God; lest any root of bitterness springing up cause trouble, and by this many become defiled...

Hebrews 12:14,15

If you forgive men their trespasses, your Heavenly Father will also forgive you. but if you do not forgive men their trespasses, neither will your father forgive your trespasses.

Matthew 6: 14,15

Whenever you stand praying, if you have anything against anyone, forgive him that your Father in heaven may also forgive your trespasses.

Mark 11:25

Therefore, as the elect of God, holy and beloved, put-on tender mercies, kindness, humility, meekness, longsuffering: bearing with one another and forgiving one another. If anyone has a complaint against another, even as Christ forgave you, so you also must do.

Colossians 4:12,13

Be kind to one another, tenderhearted, forgiving one another, as God in Christ forgave you.

Ephesians 4:32

Pray this prayer:

Father, part of Jesus' last words to you on the Cross was, "Forgive them, for they know not what they do."

This is one of the greatest lessons we could ever learn but often difficult. Help us to soften our hearts to be pliable to receive joy in the place of bitterness, peace in the place of chaos, wholeness in the place of hurt. Help us remember the Lord Jesus calling out from the Cross to forgive us. He interceded for us on the Cross that we might be able to grasp the dynamics of forgiveness and learn how to intercede for one another.

We pray to see clearly that others are not always out to hurt us, but many times Satan interferes to bring confusion to relationships. Help us to stay vigilant so as not to entertain the enemy's attempt to bring confusion. We know unforgiveness hinders our prayers. Take the bitterness away that we may serve you properly.

In Jesus's name, Amen.

The Spirit of Fear

W e are to fear the Lord in reverence and righteousness, with holy fear which keeps us near to God so that we might not fall prey to the enemy's schemes. In contrast, the *spirit of fear* is a vice that Satan uses to keep us in bondage. These are two different uses of the same word—fear.

Remember, we talked about how Adam and Eve were afraid when God called out to them in the garden. Not only did Adam and Eve feel guilt and shame about their disobedience and nakedness, but the Bible says they were afraid, so they hid (Genesis 3:8).

Adam and Eve's fear was thrust upon them by their lust and desire for fruit that God had forbidden them to eat. Satan questioned their integrity, played upon their weakness, and made the fruit appealing to them in his attempt to gain authority. Their fear was a result of unrighteous conduct and not understanding the consequences of their disobedience. We see here the lack of faith in what God had told them to do. "To eat of all the trees in the garden except the tree of knowledge of good and evil" (Genesis 2:17).

It's important to have faith in God and what He says. His commands might appear unrealistic, and perhaps even cruel, but we must strive to stay focused on truth. Ephesians 9:27 reminds us to not give place to the devil. Playing the fear card is his greatest weapon against us. He wants us to walk through this life trembling and fearful of everything so we won't see clearly on how to function in God's Kingdom. Whatever is causing fear in your life, let it go! Rebuke fear in the name of Jesus! Call it out and renounce! It's not of God.

The many facets of fear can range from timidity to the fear of dying. Fear can be the culprit for many ailments in our bodies. Some individuals will imprison themselves rather than ask God for healing. There are many missed opportunities, due to fear or timidity. Many people are fearful of the unknown, including the terror of unseen forces, even when there's no obvious threat.

As I shared in the introduction, my fear of having another stroke, the obsessive way I checked my blood pressure throughout the day, and how I scrutinized every morsel of food that I ate, held me in bondage. Thank God, He healed me of the sickness and delivered me from the fears that had come upon me as a result of the sickness.

Long before that, I was mildly timid and had developed a lack of assertiveness. It wasn't until our daughter was born with a diagnosis of Down Syndrome that I learned to speak up. I've had to advocate for her throughout the years in the area of education, employment, and other situations. Today, by the grace of God, she's a prayer warrior, supermarket greeter, and well known at church and in the community. She is aware of her diagnosis, but also believes prayer is the answer when she runs into difficulty.

The Lord opened my eyes to see that my timidity was not from Him and that I needed to trust and not limit God by making the thing about my own ability or what people might think. We can hide out and refuse to get involved, or we can step out and do what He calls us to do.

Our daughter has done everything from dancing school to attending a program at Pensacola State College where she learned life skills and made lifelong friends. She will pray for you and will want to add you to her prayer list. She loves reading the Bible and leading our at-home Bible studies.

Don't let the spirit of fear rob you of lovely, God-filled experiences. Step up and speak out. Go to the altar for prayer, lift your hands and praise God. Share your faith and let God bless you in ways such as you've never known.

We're discussing fears here that are relatively simple, but of course there are those who struggle with life-threatening concerns. There's nothing too hard for God. Whether it's about feeling timid, or fear of something extreme, let God turn your life around. Receive your healing. Receive your blessing. Don't let the enemy steal another minute of your God-given calling.

Don't be hindered or crippled by fear. Trust God and move past your circumstance to find healing in your body, mind, and spirit. Rely on these Scriptures as you are set free from fear.

For God has not given us a spirit of fear, but of power and of love and of a sound mind.

2 Timothy 1:7

There is no fear in love; but perfect love casts out fear, because fear involves torment. But he who fears has not been made perfect in love. We love Him because He first loved us.

1 John 4:18,19

For you did not receive the spirit of bondage again to fear, but you received the Spirit of adoption by whom we cry out, "Abba, Father."

Romans 8:15

So that we may boldly say, the Lord is my helper, and I will not fear what man shall do to me.

Hebrews 13:6

So do not fear, for I am with you. do not be dismayed for I am your God. I will strengthen you and help you; I will uphold you with My righteous hand.

Isaiah 40:10

Pray this prayer:

Lord, it's a great day when we trust in you. It's a glorious time when we put aside our worries and cast our cares upon you. Help us not to walk about with the spirit of fear, but to walk in full assurance of your presence knowing that if you are for us then who can be against us. You have given your angels charge over us and your word tells us you will never leave us nor forsake us. We rebuke the spirit of fear, and we receive deliverance. We call forth faith that we might be healed!

In Jesus' name, Amen.

Stress and Worry

S tress and worry can affect the entire body and disrupt a person's lifestyle in many ways—from inflammation and heart trouble, to poor eating habits and lack of sleep. Stress and worry are habits that have been adopted and have become natural behavior patterns for many in our present culture. It's become so normal that many don't even realize that they are stressed.

This behavior detaches us from God because we believe that we must go at it alone; that the power to change our situation lies only with us. Even when we do know that everything is with God and of God, we still continue to worry. We often find that it's difficult to be still and trust God.

Stress and worry are two of the most common demons that can send us to an early grave. Let's follow God's instructions and allow Jesus to take control so that we may rest and enjoy the ride.

Be anxious for nothing, but in everything by prayer and supplication, with thanksgiving, let your request be made known to God; and the peace of God, which surpasses all understanding, will guard your hearts and minds through Christ Jesus.

Philippians 4:6

Therefore, I say to you, "do not worry about your life, what you will eat or what you will drink; nor about your body, what you will put on. Is not life more than food and the body more than clothing? But seek first the Kingdom of God and his righteousness and all these things will be added to you."

Matthew 6:25,33

Casting all your care upon Him, for He cares for you.

1 Peter 1:7

But those who wait on the lord shall renew their strength: they shall mount up with wings of eagles, they shall run and not be weary they shall walk and not faint.

Isaiah 40:31

Pray this prayer:

Heavenly Father, you encourage us to trust in you with all our hearts and lean not to our own understanding. There are times of weaknesses when we are challenged in this area, where it becomes difficult to let go and relinquish our tight control over certain situations in life. Help us to live by your encouraging promises that remind us you are near to all who call on you.

Your Word tells us that you will instruct and guide us. May we hear your voice and listen to your instructions. We pray for confidence that you will see us through difficult times, because you also remind us that when we first seek your kingdom and your righteousness, you will provide our needs. Help us to surrender all and to trust you that we might turn our worries into victories of strength and healing.

In Jesus' name, Amen.

Discouragement, Disappointment, or Bitterness

I t may happen that if a person is not instantly healed when prayed for, they allow discouragement, disappointment, or bitterness to come in. It will be difficult to receive answers to prayers if disappointment is entertained. The enemy can come in with a lie that no healing took place, when, in fact, it might be a situation of a gradual healing for God's own purpose.

We must hold on with full assurance, trusting in God. Continue to declare healing! Don't facilitate discouragement, ignorance, deception, or anger by allowing it to find a place in your heart. Guard your heart from these things. Talk to God to find the intimacy needed to keep peace in your life as you navigate the process of waiting. Lean not to your own understanding (Proverbs 3:5). Examine yourself to know whether your own behavior might be contributing to your delayed healing. Pray for spiritual wisdom.

Also, during prayer, activate your faith. Work with the person who is praying for you. Mix faith with your petition. Remember the widow of Zarephath and the prophet Elijah. They each brought something to the table, and both were able to partake (1 Kings 17).

If you've done all you know to do, trust God! Don't overthink it, just rest in Jesus. Stay vigilant, not passive, continuing in faith and believing God's promises. Don't get hung up as Naaman, the leper, did in 2 Kings 5:10-12. He had difficulty receiving instructions for his healing from the prophet, Elisha.

The prophet's words made no sense to Naaman. Elisha's instruction to Naaman was to "go and wash in the Jordan seven times, and your flesh shall be restored to you, and you shall be clean."

But Naaman became furious, and went away and said, "Indeed, I said to myself, 'He will surely come out to me, and stand and call on the name of the Lord his God, and wave his hand over the place, and heal the leprosy.' Are not the Abanah and the Pharpar, the rivers of Damascus, better than all the waters of Israel? Could I not wash in them and be clean?" So he turned and went away in a rage.

2 Kings 5:10-12

Naaman believed he needed to hear the prophet say words of wisdom and do some sort of ritual for his healing to be authentic. Naaman's servant convinced him to obey the prophet and he was healed!

Try not to get caught up in the dynamics of how healing will be manifested. Focus on obedience to God's Word and believe.

Now to him who is able to do exceedingly abundantly above all that we ask or think, according to the power that works in us, to Him be glory in the church by Christ Jesus unto all generations, forever and ever. Amen.

Ephesians 3:20-21

That you put off, concerning your former conduct, the old man which grows corrupt according to your deceitful lusts, and be renewed in the spirit of your mind, and that you put on the new man which was created according to God, in true righteousness and holiness.

Ephesians 4:22-24

The lord makes firm the steps of the one who delights in him; though he may stumble, he will not fall, for the lord upholds with his hand.

Psalms 37:23,24

In my distress, I called to the lord, and he answered me.

Psalms 120:1

We need the Lord to give us the wisdom that the apostle Paul shared as he prayed for the people at Ephesus.

That the God of our lord Jesus Christ, the father of glory, may give to you the spirit of wisdom and revelation in the knowledge of him, the eyes of your understanding being enlightened; that you may know what is the hope of that calling, what are the riches of the glory of his inheritance in the saints, and what is the exceeding greatness of his power toward us who believe according to the working of his mighty power which he worked in Christ when he raised him from the dead and seated him at his right hand in the heavenly places, far above principality and power and might and dominion.

Ephesians 1:17-21

Pray this prayer:

Father, I pray for any who are holding hurt, bitterness, disappointment, discouragement or anger. That You would give wisdom and discernment to see how to move forward, opening their eyes and hearts to joyfully receive answers to prayers according to your way.

We know that it is your will that all are healed. We pray to learn to wait on You Lord because there's powerful growth and healing in the process of waiting for our loving Father. We understand that many times You are waiting for us to be transformed by the renewing of our minds. Help us to not let previous experiences and deceptions interfere with our ability to receive healing on this day.

In Jesus' name, Amen

Self-Reliance

When we try to make decisions independent of God, we invite trouble as David did with the census. Although David was a man after God's heart he, at times, misjudged situations (1 Samuel 13:14). Whether it be regarding pride, complacency, or lust, God is a God of justice and correction which is essential for proper spiritual growth. We need to consider the consequences before we try going it alone. Jesus is our source! Depend on him!

In the book of Genesis, there's a man named Nimrod of whom the Bible tells us was a mighty hunter before the lord. A literal hunter and leader but also a tyrant who brought self-reliance to the level of defiance (Genesis 10:8-10).

He gathered men to work against God by building the infamous Tower of Babel. At that time the people had one language. The beginning of one his kingdoms was Babel. Nimrod's goal was to build this tower independent of God.

> *Come let us build ourselves a city, and a tower whose top is in the heavens; let us make a name for ourselves, lest we be scattered abroad over the face of the earth. The Lord came down and confused their language and scattered them abroad over the face of the earth.*
>
> Genesis 11:1-9

It's important for us to consult with our Father God when making decisions, and not try to go around Him to accomplish the thing. Learn to lean on God, and trust in Him for the answer.

> *For by grace, you have been saved and that not of yourselves; it is the gift of God, not of works, lest anyone should boast.*
>
> Ephesians 2:8

Not that we are sufficient in ourselves to claim anything as coming from us, but our sufficiency is from God.

2 Corinthians 3:5

Be anxious for nothing, but in everything by prayer and supplication, with thanksgiving, let your request be made known to God.

Philippians 4:6

I am the vine, you are the branches, he who abides in Me, and I, in him, bears much fruit; for, without Me you can do nothing.

John 15:5

Pray this prayer:

We have a tendency, Lord, to get carried away with ideas and ideals that we think might be beneficial to whatever aspirations or goals we're trying to achieve. Often, we want to go to it on our own and find ourselves in precarious situations filled with anxieties and mental anguish. Whether it be pride, foolishness, complacency, or ignorance, at the end of the day, we need You for all of life's situations.

Your Word tells us that all things are for you, through you and to you to Whom be glory forever. We give you glory and honor, Lord. We magnify Your Holy name as we lift up the name of Jesus. We pray that we're not so anxious or prideful that we forget to seek counsel from you. We know you want us to be strong, make wise decisions, and do as much as we can for ourselves, but there are times when we need to consult with you to know how to proceed in the handling of certain matters of ministry, stewarding, sickness, family, or relational.

Help us to recognize that no matter the task, we need you. Humble our hearts that we might endeavor to seek you and depend on your wisdom to instruct us and guide in all things. We pray the Holy Spirit will help us to discern the difference between doing all that we can do and depending on You for the other part.

In Jesus' name, Amen.

Disobedience and Sin

We know it was disobedience and sin by Adam and Eve that led to the uncovering of man's sin nature; a rebellion that we were never supposed to see or know. This rebellion continues today with the help of Satan as in the beginning.

Be sober, be vigilant because your adversary the devil walks about like a roaring lion, seeking whom he may devour.

1 Peter 5:8

Therefore, submit to God, resist the devil and he will flee from you.

James 4:7

For the wages of sin is death, but the gift of God is eternal life in Christ Jesus our lord.

Romans 6:23

But Peter and the other disciples answered and said: "we ought to obey God rather than men."

Acts 5:29

"But why do you call me Lord, Lord and not do the things which I say?"

Luke 6:46

Pray this prayer:

Today we call out rebellion. We say that greater is He who lives in us than he who is in the world (1 John 4:4). We pray Lord, that we're able to activate the authority you have given us to bind evil thoughts, temptations, or impulses. When the enemy brings temptation and deceptions, we ask for strength to guard against wrong doings as we continue to resist the tactics and traps from the enemy.

We pray to be able to put on our spiritual armor that we may be able to stand against the wiles of the devil (Ephesians 6:11). Scripture teaches us not to deviate from your Word, for in doing so, it could lead to all sorts of adversities including sickness and disease.

We pray that we would be sensitive to the warnings of our Counselor, the Holy Spirit, to enable us to be conscious of the oppressing strategies of Satan. We can become overcomers who are not bound up in sin, disobedience, and sickness.

We know we're not perfect and there are times where we will sin, but your Word tells us not to engage in a life of sin (a continuous pattern of sinful behavior). We pray for wisdom to make right choices, obeying your Word and walking in peace that we may spend eternity in your presence.

In Jesus' name, Amen.

Demonic Oppression

The Bible tells us there are demonic forces constantly warring against us. We may unconsciously open doors to these forces when we become involved or participate in evil influences. On the other hand, these forces may have been involuntarily thrust upon a person through outside experiences, such as physical, emotional, or sexual abuse. Whatever the circumstances, Satan will use these to torment by inflicting shame and guilt.

Such evil forces bring all manner of chaos and disruption into a believer's existence, such as encouraging defiance, rebellion, and possibly shattering God-relationships.

In the case of unbelievers, there's an attempt to further remove any possibility of knowing Jesus. These encounters with demonic forces will attack our bodies, causing all kinds of sicknesses. We don't always understand the source of many illnesses. Some can be traced back to demonic oppression where Satan used unresolved issues of shame, guilt, or outright defiance, to strike us with sicknesses. It's important to contact a church leader, or a professional Christian counselor, to get help with issues of demonic attacks.

God has made provision for us to be able to resolve sickness, even when it stems from attacks from the enemy. In the case of an assault (you did nothing to bring on the attack), ask God to help you find the peace and strength needed to move forward and to receive your healing. The shed blood of Jesus brings victory for all. We don't have to be hampered by oppression of any kind.

However, when a person voluntarily opens the door of sinful behavior, there must be repentance and a turning away from sin in order for closure to occur.

As believers, we have the authority to declare God's Words and promises over our lives. Be strong and recognize the power God has given you to rise up receive your inheritance and your identity in Jesus. Proclaim victory over the enemy's strategies against you.

And behold, there was a woman who had a spirit of infirmity eighteen years. and was bent over and could in no way raise herself up. But when Jesus saw her, He called her to Him and said to her, "woman, you are loosed from your infirmity." He laid his hand on her, and immediately she was made straight, and glorified God. The ruler of the synagogue became indignant because Jesus healed the woman on the Sabbath. Jesus answered, saying "Ought not this woman, being a daughter of Abraham, whom Satan has bound for eighteen years be loosed from this bond on the Sabbath?"

Luke 13:11-16

You know of Jesus of Nazareth, how God anointed Him with the Holy Spirit and with power, and how He went about doing good and healing all who were oppressed by the devil, for God was with Him.

Acts 10:38

For we do not wrestle against flesh and blood, but against principalities, against powers, against the rulers of the darkness of this age, against spiritual hosts of wickedness in the heavenly places.

Ephesians 6:12

Pray this prayer:

Lord, when we're faced with battling wicked principalities, we're quickly reminded of just how much we need you. The blood of Jesus is always the answer. When you were living as a man on the earth, you told us you would not leave us as orphans. That after your ascension, you would send the Holy Spirit to be our Helper. Thank you for our Helper who lives in us and gives us power and authority to heal in Jesus' name.

As believers, we say that demonic oppression has no legal right to intrude or invade our territory. You told us not to give the devil a place (Ephesians 4:27). We pray for clarity in recognizing the enemy's attempt to sow conflict in our spirit and bodies. We pray for wholeness in every area of our bodies where sickness may have occurred as a result of demonic oppression.

We thank you for your Word which encourages us to continue to seek answers and find hope in whatever challenges we might come against. We pray for deliverance, and a fresh anointing and boldness.

In Jesus' name, Amen.

Other Strongholds

There are areas in our lives where Satan might have a firm grip—a hook which gives rise to certain urges, tendencies, and impulses. Perhaps it's due to a traumatic incident which might have contributed to these behavioral patterns. The enemy will try to convince you that you need to engage in ungodly behavior in order to quell or pacify these urges. These are strongholds. They are like fortified walls of deception, that Satan has erected to hold you hostage. He wants to keep you mentally incarcerated and sentence you to a life of dependency. Satan's goal is to induce habitual behavior that's rooted in pride and self-destruction while raising haughty arguments against God.

These behaviors include:
1. Addictions (drugs, alcohol, gambling, overeating)
2. Constant worrying
3. Succumbing to negative generational models, for instance, "My whole family had colon cancer; I'm no different. It won't be long before I'm diagnosed with colon cancer too." The blood of Jesus changes your DNA. It is up to you to receive Christ's identity by faith, and affect change for your family.
4. Incessant complaining
5. Hate and racism
6. Idolatry (anything and everything that comes before God)
7. Pornography
8. A spirit of anger and violence
9. Slander and gossip

This certainly is not a complete list, but these give a clear picture that Satan wants to rule and reign in various parts of a person's life. You can make a decision today that you are ready to put an end to the enemy's intrusion. Take back control of your life through the power of the blood of Jesus.

It's only through Jesus and His finished work at the Cross that we can renew our minds in the newness of our Lord and Savior. Be filled with His Holy Spirit that you might take authority over your body and

> 164

mind to proclaim, "I can do all things through Christ who strengthens me" (Philippians 4:13).

If you are not a believer in Jesus and would like to receive Him, you can do that now. Pray this prayer for salvation:

"Father, I know you sent Your Son to the world to die for me and to set me free. Forgive my sins as I confess Jesus as my Lord and Savior. I invite Jesus to live in my heart. Thank you, Father, for Your loving kindness toward me and for the gift of salvation."

You can use these Scriptures to help you in your walk with the Lord.

Wine is a mocker. Strong drink is a brawler, and whoever is led astray by it is not wise.

Proverbs 20:1

Come to me, all you who labor and are heavy laden, and I will give you rest.

Matthew 11:28

All things are lawful for me, but all things are not helpful. All things are lawful for me, but I will not be brought under the power of any.

1 Corinthians 6:12

For though we walk in the flesh, we do not war according to the flesh. for the weapons of our warfare are not carnal but mighty in God for pulling down strongholds, casting down arguments and every high thing that exalts itself against the knowledge of God, bringing every thought into captivity to the obedience of Christ.

2 Corinthians 10:3-5

Therefore we also, since we are surrounded by so great a cloud of witnesses, let us lay aside every weight, and the sin which so easily ensnares us and let us run with endurance the race that is set before us, looking unto Jesus, the author and finisher of our faith, who for the joy that was set before Him endured the cross, despising the shame, and has sat down at the right hand of the throne of God.

Hebrews 12:1,2

Pray this prayer:

Lord, I am bound by chains that only you can break; unseen forces that drive me to engage in what seem to be uncontrollable habits. I recognize these habits are destructive. I know my strength is in you. However, when the temptation to succumb settles over me, I feel overwhelmed to satisfy the urge which results in adverse actions.

I need You, Lord! I pray for guidance and direction. I pray to be able to walk in the Spirit as opposed to the flesh. The dynamics of this battle are great and who can count the tremendous consequences.

Holy Spirit, help me in this battle, help me to begin the process of opening my mind and heart to a new life. A life where I can be the servant I have been called to be without the limits that come as a result of weakness, external influences, and not abiding in Your truths. I pray to be established and settled in my identity, completely equipped and strengthened to stand firm against interferences of any kind. The power that lives in me is the same power that raised Jesus from the dead. I have the authority to cast down strongholds and every evil thing.

In Jesus' name, Amen.

General Barriers

L ike the person who is discouraged because an instant healing was not received, you might feel apprehensive about stepping out for prayer for the first time. Maybe you feel embarrassed about the attention that sometimes comes with public prayer, not wanting to be judged by onlookers.

Again, don't let the devil deceive you. Step out there, ask for, and receive the prayers. Don't limit God. He wants you healed!

Part III

Believe and Receive Your Healing

Throughout *Healing in His Wings: Honoring and Embracing God's Promises,* the truth has been presented that it is the will of God to heal all who believe. Mark 11:24 says whatever things you ask for when you pray, believe that you receive them, and you will have them. Also, we mustn't forget about verses 25 and 26 which makes it clear that forgiveness is imperative.

In grasping God's truth regarding healing, it's important to see that throughout the Word, there is a wide variety of patterns. No matter whether a person is in the process of a gradual healing (Luke 17:14, Mark 8:22-25, 2 Kings 5:10), or an instant manifestation (Mark 2:1-12, Mark 10:46-52), God wants His children to be whole, well and healthy!

Proclaim God's Word for Healing

Perhaps your healing will come by **proclaiming God's Word** over your sickness as recorded in 1 Peter 2:24. Or it may come by the **laying on of hands** as seen in Matthew 9:18,25, Matthew 19:13-15, and Mark 16:18. Perhaps **by faith** you have received your supernatural healing, similar to the woman with the issue of blood in

Mark 5:25-34. Or perhaps you are **agreeing in prayer** with someone according to Matthew 18:19 and James 5:16.

Taking authority in the name of Jesus is powerful!

And these signs will follow those who believe, in my name they will cast out demons, they will speak with new tongues, they will take up serpents: and if they drink anything deadly, it will by no means hurt them. They will lay hands on the sick and they will recover.

Mark 16:17-18.

Additionally, Jesus tells his disciples in Luke 24:49, "Behold I send the promise of my father upon you: but tarry in the city of Jerusalem until you are endued with power from on high."

Soul Winning

Soul winning offers a wide range of signs and wonders. When we minister to others, the Lord is working with us to confirm the Word through accompanying signs (Mark 16:20). We find supernatural strength when we commit to sharing God's Word.

They shall bear fruit in old age; they shall be fresh and flourishing; to declare that the Lord is upright.

Psalm 92:14-15

Praise Your Way to Healing

It's possible that you might **praise your way** to your healing. King Jehoshaphat had worshippers praise God to win their battle.

And when he had consulted with the people, he appointed those who should sing to the Lord, and who should praise the beauty of holiness, as they went out before the army and were saying: "Praise the Lord, For His mercy endures forever."

Now when they began to sing and to praise, the Lord set ambushes against the people of Ammon, Moab, and Mount Seir, who had come against Judah; and they were defeated.

2 Chronicles 20:21,22

The Medical Community for Healing

In addition to all these methods of healing, God has given us the medical community. In his love and compassion, He knows that many have not come to recognize or understand the exchange that transpired at the Cross where Jesus took our sins and gave us His peace. Even when we do understand, we have difficulty absorbing it all, especially upon receiving a scary medical diagnosis.

It's a natural inclination to choose to go to the hospital or clinic. God put these resources in place for us, knowing that we may have difficulty utilizing what He made available for us through the shed blood of Jesus. He cares for our well-being and expects us to know the truth of His Word. Build your faith and believe God for your healing.

"Woe to the rebellious children," says the Lord, "Who take counsel, but not of Me, And who devise plans, but not of My Spirit, That they may add sin to sin; Who walk to go down to Egypt, And have not asked My advice, To strengthen themselves in the strength of Pharaoh, And to trust in the shadow of Egypt!"

Isaiah 30:1,2

Going to Egypt, represents a type of returning to worldliness for answers to your problems. An example is King Asa in the Old Testament.

And in the thirty-ninth year of his reign, Asa became diseased in his feet, and his malady was severe; yet in his disease he did not seek the LORD, but the physicians.

2 Chronicles 16:12

Matthew 6:33 tells us to seek first the Kingdom of God and His righteousness, and all *these things* will be added to us. We're to not worry because then we would be like the unbelievers (Verses 31,32).

God, in His sovereignty, might direct you go to the hospital for healing and recovery. There is nothing wrong with that, but be sure to seek Him, and trust in Him to help you know how to navigate. Maintain a posture of faith. Thank God for the medical community and the many healings that have occurred as a result of their commitment, work, and God-given wisdom.

Believe and Receive

Of course, obedience, the fear of the Lord, and all that has been discussed previously, opens windows of opportunities for us to receive our healings.

The point here is that no matter what the method of healing, our part is to believe and receive by faith. We honor God for the work that has been already done. Our lives and our actions must reflect gratitude, praise, worship, glory, commitment, and good stewardship. We first believe God's Word, which means we believe it's His will for all of His children to be healed.

Declare God's Holy Word and promises over your life and live your life to honor what has already been given. Then praise and honor your Father in heaven for He is worthy of all praise!

Conclusion

"I am the Alpha and the Omega, the Beginning and the End," says the Lord, "who is and who was and who is to come, the Almighty."

Revelation 1:8

The book of Revelation gives us a glimpse of heavenly rejoicing and praise. From the four living creatures, to the twenty-four elders, then to the angels, all are worshipping God and Jesus on the throne.

Great and marvelous are Your works,
Lord God Almighty!
Just and true are Your ways,
O King of the saints!
Who shall not fear You, O Lord, and glorify Your name?
For You alone are holy.
For all nations shall come and worship before You,
For Your judgments have been manifested.

Revelation 15:3,4

And every creature which is in heaven and on the earth and under the earth and such as are in the sea, and all that are in them, I heard saying: "Blessing and honor and glory and power Be to Him who sits on the throne, And to the Lamb, forever and ever!"

Revelation 5:13

Jesus is the only One found worthy to receive the scrolls and open the seals. The seals represent cycles of judgement that will come upon the earth in the final days.

You are worthy to take the scroll,

And to open its seals;

For You were slain,

And have redeemed us to God by Your blood

Out of every tribe and tongue and people and nation,

And have made us kings and priests to our God;

And we shall reign on the earth.

Revelation 5:9,10

The message of the Gospel is for all people, nations, and tongues. The gift of salvation (deliverance from sin and its consequences) is for all.

My little children, these things I write to you, so that you may not sin. And if anyone sins, we have an Advocate with the Father, Jesus Christ the righteous. and He Himself is the propitiation for our sins: and not for ours only, but for the sins of the whole world.

1 John 2:1,2

Psalm 103:5 tells us He forgives all our iniquities and heals all our diseases. The Prophet Isaiah reminds us that Jesus was bruised for our iniquities; the chastisement for our peace was upon Him and by His stripes, we are healed (Isaiah 53:5). Peter reinforces these truths when he declares in 1 Peter 2:24, "Who Himself bore our sins in His own body on the tree, that we, having died to sins, might live for righteousness—by whose stripes you were healed."

And then in Proverbs we learn that God's Word is life and health.

My son, give attention to my words; Incline your ear to my sayings. Do not let them depart from your eyes; Keep them in the midst of your heart; For they are life to those who find them, And health to all their flesh.

Proverbs 4:20-22

Because we have been transformed by the blood of Jesus, we can walk in faith and activate God's promises of healing. We can thank Him and praise Him for He has done great things.

The book of Malachi ends with God taking notice of the remnant of believers waiting for the first coming of King Jesus.

But to you who fear My name The Sun of Righteousness shall arise with healing in His wings; And you shall go out And grow fat like stall-fed calves. You shall trample the wicked, For they shall be ashes under the soles of your feet On the day that I do this," Says the Lord of hosts.

Malachi 4:2,3

Today, let us continue strong and in good health, planting seeds, and watering like the remnant of Malachi's day, as we patiently wait for His second return.

The Lord is not slack concerning His promise, as some count slackness, but is patient toward us, not willing that any should perish but that all should come to repentance.

2 Peter 3:9

Pray this prayer:

Father, we honor you, we praise you, we love you. May your mercy endure forever. The redeemed here on earth bow down to worship you, just as the host of heaven. As we come before you, we thank you that you are longsuffering and that you are the God who forgives.

We pray that the Holy Spirit would help us to learn obedience so that we may partake fully of all the blessings you have graciously bestowed upon us. We love your instructions, guidance, and correction.

We pray that our faith is strong as Abraham's. We call out to You as did blind Bartimaeus and we throw off hindrances, just as he threw off his cloak. We hear Your Word, and we touch the hem of Your garment by believing what we have heard. We put You first like the widow of Zarephath who otherwise would not have had enough food for her and her son to live; but the prophet Elijah encouraged her to not fear.

We find joy, gladness and rejoicing in serving You. We are thankful, because Your Word teaches us about thanksgiving from the Psalms of David to the lesson of the ten lepers. where the one Samaritan came back to thank You as he walked in faith (Luke 17:11-19).

Today we walk in that same faith. We trust Your Holy Word as we receive our healing and we, also, say Thank You!

In Jesus name, Amen.

I trust that as you have read *Healing in His Wings: Honoring and Embracing God's Promises*, you have gained fresh insight in that it is definitely God's will for all to be whole, well, and healthy, and that there are many methods for receiving healing. We are to be bold in our love for God and bold in our love for one another. And bold to come before the Throne of Grace and receive all that is provided to each believer. That includes divine health and healing.

About the Author

Patricia Simon

In 2008, Patricia Simon was healed from a stroke. However, the prescribed blood pressure medicine worked to keep her sick. After ten years of misery, God delivered her from the medicine. Once free, she immersed herself in healing scriptures and was both stunned and conflicted to see that the attitude of other believer's and their response regarding sickness seldom lined up with God's Word. During her recuperation, she developed a passion for Scripture and began teaching weekly Bible classes at her church.

Patricia was later inspired to begin a healing class to gain understanding of the disconnect between sickness among believers and the truth of God's Word. She decided to write out a synopsis for guidance and scriptural references. That

Patricia Simon

synopsis morphed into this book, *Healing in His Wings: Honoring and Embracing God's Promises.*

Patricia is an author and a life-group leader at her church in Hammond, LA. She is passionate for the Word of God and has a zeal for soul winning.

www.ingramcontent.com/pod-product-compliance
Lightning Source LLC
La Vergne TN
LVHW051057080426
835508LV00019B/1925